Roman Roads
and Aqueducts

Other titles in the *History's Great Structures* series include:

History's Great
STRUCTURES

Roman Roads
and Aqueducts

Don Nardo

ReferencePoint
Press®

San Diego, CA

© 2015 ReferencePoint Press, Inc.
Printed in the United States

For more information, contact:
ReferencePoint Press, Inc.
PO Box 27779
San Diego, CA 92198
www.ReferencePointPress.com

LIBRARY OF CONGRESS CATALOGING-IN-PUBLICATION DATA

Nardo, Don, 1947–
    [Roman Roads and aqueducts (ReferencePoint Press)]
    Roman roads and aqueducts / by Don Nardo.
      pages cm -- (History's great structures)
    Audience: Grades 9 to 12.
    Includes bibliographical references and index.
      ISBN 978-1-60152-634-2 (hardback) -- ISBN 1-60152-634-2 (hardback)
  1. Roads, Roman--Juvenile literature. 2. Transportation--Rome--Juvenile literature.
  3. Aqueducts--Rome--Juvenile literature. 4. Water-supply--Rome--Juvenile literature.
  5. Rome--Antiquities--Juvenile literature. I. Title.
    DG28.N3725   2014
    388.1'0937--dc23
                                                                    2013031024

CONTENTS

IMPORTANT EVENTS IN THE HISTORY OF ROMAN ROADS AND AQUEDUCTS

CA. 500s
The Persians build their Royal Road, stretching from what is now southern Iraq to western Turkey.

272
The Romans begin building another aqueduct, the Aqua Anio, to supply parts of the capital with water.

CA. 753
The traditional date for the city of Rome's founding.

18
The aqueduct today called the Pont du Gard, created to bring water to what is now the French city of Nimes, is completed.

BCE 750   500   250   CE

CA. 509–30
The years of the Roman Republic, in which Rome is ruled by representatives of the people.

38–52
The years during which one of Rome's most magnificent aqueducts—the Aqua Claudia—is built.

312
Work begins on Rome's first major highway, the Via Appia. Construction also starts on Rome's first aqueduct, the Aqua Appia.

97
Sextus Julius Frontinus becomes the city of Rome's water commissioner and overseer of the aqueducts. He begins writing a detailed book about Rome's water system.

1988
The Italians dedicate a picturesque national park situated along a stretch of the ancient Via Appia.

206
The city of Rome is now supplied by eleven aqueducts.

410
The Romans are forced to abandon their province of Britain, but the roads there subsequently remain in use for many years.

1453
Pope Nicholas V renovates the Aqua Virgo aqueduct, which serves Rome. He renames the structure the Aqua Vergine.

1943
During World War II German armies march down the Via Appia on their way to counterattack the invading Allies.

500   1000   1500   2000

1924
Italian composer Ottorino Respighi writes *The Pines of Rome*, a large-scale orchestral work that depicts events along the ancient Via Appia.

476
The last Roman emperor is forced from his throne, and the Roman imperial government ceases to exist.

2006
A major corporation grants funding to repair and maintain the imposing Roman aqueduct serving the Spanish town of Segovia.

CA. 300
The Roman Empire now has some 370 paved or partially paved highways.

Making a Great Empire Possible

Today when someone mentions ancient roads or aqueducts (channels that carry water to cities), most people think about the ones built by the Romans, long-ago masters of the Italian peninsula. This is only natural and fitting. After all, these structures were among the finest construction works that ancient Rome produced, and the Romans were far and away the greatest builders of the ancient world. Their roads and aqueducts, several of which remain in amazingly good condition, are a testament to the genius of that vanished people.

More than anything else, many historians have suggested, a strong tendency toward practicality characterized the inherent Roman genius. That is, their remarkable talent for solving practical problems—both simple and complex—was the driving force behind much of what they achieved. In this view, the true Roman artist was not a sculptor, painter, actor, or poet. Instead, the chief Roman art was engineering. "Roman genius was called into action by the enormous practical needs of a world empire," the late, renowned scholar Edith Hamilton stated. She added that Rome met these needs in part by creating an enormous system of roads. "The mighty Roman road," she wrote, was "a monument of dogged, unconquerable human effort." This, indeed, was "the true art of Rome."[1]

Earlier Road Systems

The Romans did not actually invent roads and aqueducts. Nor did they originate religious temples, palaces, town halls, racetracks, theaters, or many other monumental, or large-scale, structures they erected across their vast realm. Various earlier peoples had such structures well before the Romans arrived on the scene.

Large-scale roads, for example, were first engineered by the Assyrians. A warlike people who dwelled in Mesopotamia, what is now Iraq, they built a network of roads in the late second millennium (the 1000s) BCE. That was several centuries before Rome's traditional founding date of 753 BCE.

The Assyrian roads were composed mainly of hard-packed earth. A number of short stretches, however—those leading up to temples and other key buildings—were paved. The method of this paving was to lay down a layer or two of kiln-fired bricks and to place on top of them thick slabs of polished limestone.

A few centuries later, when Rome was still a small, dirty town with no paved roads, another Middle Eastern people, the Persians, ruled Mesopotamia along with their homeland—what is now Iran. The Persians wisely maintained and over time expanded the existing Assyrian roads. One of these expansions was Persia's famous Royal Road. It ran for more than 1,600 miles (2,575 km) eastward from the Mediterranean coast to the Persian capital of Susa. The fifth-century-BCE Greek historian Herodotus actually traveled on the Royal Road. In his book, the world's first known history text, he described it, saying, "At intervals all along the road are recognized stations, with excellent inns, and the road itself is safe to travel by, as it never leaves inhabited country." About the highway's length, Herodotus wrote:

> If the measurement of the road in parasangs is correct, and if a parasang is equal, as indeed it is, to 30 furlongs [about 3.8

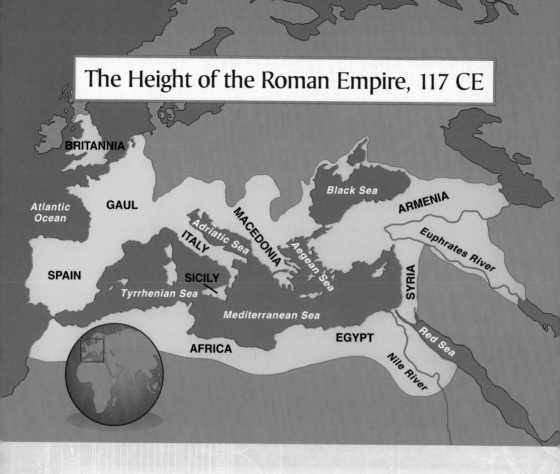

The Height of the Roman Empire, 117 CE

miles or 6 km], then the distance from Sardis [a city in what is now Turkey] to the palace [in Susa]—450 parasangs—will be 13,500 furlongs [about 1,688 miles or 2,704 km]. Traveling, then, at the rate of 150 furlongs [about 19 miles or 30 km] a day, a man will take just ninety days to make the journey.[2]

Dwarfed by Rome

The Greeks and some other ancient peoples also constructed roads, as well as aqueducts. But for quality—and especially in sheer numbers—all of the pre-Roman road systems and water channels were quite literally dwarfed by those of Rome. As they did in so many other areas, the Romans borrowed the best ideas of their neighbors and predecessors. They then skillfully combined them with their own native concepts and abilities to create things that were extremely practical, efficient, and most of all, large scale. They erected buildings of tremendous size. These included, Hamilton wrote, "amphitheaters where eighty thousand could watch a spectacle, baths where three thousand could bathe at the same time, which nearly two thousand years have left practically intact."[3]

In some ways even more majestic in scope was Rome's road system. By about 300 CE the Roman Empire had a total of more than 370 at least partially paved major highways, stretching about 53,000 miles (85,295 km). In addition, there were thousands of smaller dirt roads branching out from the principal ones in Roman territory.

WORDS IN CONTEXT
furlong
A mostly antiquated measure of distance equal to about one-eighth of a modern mile (roughly 660 feet or about 201 meters).

This monumental road network was more than a marvelous engineering feat. As University of California classics professor Jo-Ann Shelton explains, it also made Rome's huge, far-flung domain—perhaps the most influential empire in world history—possible. The "problems of communication and transportation" for any large realm, she writes, were and continue to be daunting,

> The commercial and economic stability of Rome, as well as its administrative and military supremacy, depended on an efficient network of roads throughout the city itself, throughout Italy, and throughout the Empire. These well-constructed roads (many are still in use today) allowed the Romans to communicate quickly with any part of the Empire and to transport supplies, businessmen, messengers, bureaucrats, or military troops cheaply and safely.[4]

A Wonder of the World

No less important than these roads in making the gigantic Roman realm possible were its many miles of aqueducts. Those channels supplied the life-giving water crucial to sustaining hundreds of cities. The first-century-BCE Greek geographer Strabo, who lived in the capital city of Rome for some thirteen years, was awed by its aqueducts. "The quantity of water brought into the city by the aqueducts," he wrote, "is so great that rivers, as it were, flow through the city and the sewers. And almost every house has water tanks, service pipes, and plentiful streams of water."[5]

The great Roman naturalist Pliny the Elder was born about a year before Strabo died in 24 CE. In his huge, encyclopedic work, the *Natural History*, Pliny summed up the majesty of Rome's aqueducts in a statement that could have included Roman roads as well. People should "ponder" Rome's "abundant water supply," he said. "If we consider the distances traveled by the water, the building of the arches, the tunneling through mountains, and the construction of the level routes across valleys, we can only conclude that this is a supreme wonder of the world."[6] Indeed, this remains the verdict of humanity today, more than nineteen centuries after Pliny penned those words.

CHAPTER ONE

To the Edges of the World

In his surviving geography text, the ancient Greek scholar and traveler Strabo said that the Romans "were especially farsighted about matters to which the Greeks gave little thought, such as the construction of roads." As a result, he went on, the Romans "have constructed roads throughout the countryside, cutting through hills and filling in depressions, so that now their wagons can carry loads equivalent to those of boats."[7]

At the time he wrote these words, Strabo did not foresee a world in which the Roman Empire would exist only in memory and historical accounts. Yet that world did come to pass. Many centuries passed after the Roman realm collapsed, and much of what had been Roman decayed or faded away. That included the Romans' very identity. The descendants of the Empire's inhabitants came to see themselves as Italian, French, German, Spanish, and English, rather than Roman.

Still, during all those years a few Roman traits and achievements never lost their lofty reputation or luster. One was Rome's immense network of roads. Many of these remained in use for centuries, serving not only as helpful conveniences but also as reminders that a mighty civilization had once existed in Europe. As late as the twentieth century, the Roman roads were for many people an awe-inspiring accomplishment. Edith Hamilton, for one, waxed poetic. Those highways, she wrote, consisted of "huge stone jointed to huge stone, marching on and on irresistibly, through unknown hostile forests, over ramparts of mountains, across sun-baked deserts, to the very edges of the habitable world."[8]

Road Types and Names

Although the ancient Roman road system as a whole lives on as one of history's great structures, many of its details and complexities are no longer common knowledge. For example, few people today know the various kinds of roads that made up that system. In fact, like modern nations, the Roman realm had numerous different types of roads, each with a special function and a separate name.

Of those road names, the most familiar today is *via*. Rather than a term for roads in general, it identified a specific kind. Namely, a *via* was a road wide enough to accommodate two vehicles, such as wagons or chariots, at the same time—about 15 to 18 feet (4.6 to 5.5 m). It became the term most often used to describe major highways, including what is now the best known of all Rome's roads—the Via Appia, also called the Appian Way, in central Italy. (The terms *Appia* and *Appian* refer to Appius Claudius, the Roman government official who sponsored and oversaw initial construction of that highway.) Other well-known Roman *viae* included the Via Flaminia in Italy, the Via Egnatia in Greece, the Via Valeria in Sicily, and the Via Augusta in Spain.

WORDS IN CONTEXT

vicus
A city street.

The *viae* most often ran from one city or region to another. In contrast, each city had its local streets, the generic name for which was *vici*. A single city street was a *vicus*. In an average-sized town, the main *vici* could accommodate the majority of normal traffic, but most city streets were smaller—just wide enough for a farmer's wagon. In the larger cities and towns, the major streets were mainly for vehicles. Pedestrians usually walked on raised sidewalks called *crepidines*. In part this was to keep them out of the manure, rotting garbage, and other refuse routinely tossed into the streets. Many smaller towns

The Via Appia, or Appian Way, was built from smoothly fitted blocks of stone on a heavy stone foundation. One of Rome's major highways, it speeded the transport of merchandise to numerous towns in Italy.

lacked sidewalks, however. So their residents had to do the best they could to avoid whatever rubbish littered the streets.

Regarding the naming of city streets, some were labeled for professions or activities that were common on them. For instance, more than one city had a Vicus Sandalarius, or "street of the sandal makers." Another common example was the Vicus Argentarius, or "street of the money changers." Streets were also named for prominent monuments on them, like the Vicus Apollinis, or "Apollo street," after a temple of Apollo, god of prophecy and light. Still other city streets bore the names of ethnic groups whose members were numerous in the area. The Vicus Tuscus, or "Etruscan street," for instance, referred to the Etruscans, an Italian people whose lands bordered Rome during its first few centuries. A fairly large proportion of smaller streets had no names at all, which made it difficult to give a visitor directions.

Other kinds of roads also had standard names. A common example was an *angiportus*, a narrow street or alleyway. Only a few of the many others included *clivus*, meaning a roadway that sloped steeply upward; *agger*, a road running along a raised mound or causeway; *actus*, a single-lane, unpaved country road; and *limes*, a narrow dirt road that marked the boundary line between two country estates or regions.

Classifying Roads

Besides individual names for roads, the Romans assigned them general categories. These official classifications were based mainly on the individual or organization that paid for the building of the road. Historians know about these aspects of Rome's roads thanks to Siculus Flaccus, a first-century-CE Roman surveyor. He wrote a book listing four official road classifications that existed in his time.

The first category of road Flaccus mentioned is *viae publicae*, meaning public highways. They were financed and built by the central government and bore "the names of their builders." Also, Flaccus wrote, public highways "are under the charge of administrators, who have the work done by contractors. For some of these roads, the landowners in the area are required, too, from time to time, to pay a fixed sum."[9]

WORDS IN CONTEXT
viae publicae
Public highways.

The administrators maintained the public roads. These individuals differed according to the era in which they lived, as well as the particular job they did. During the era of the Roman Republic, a period that spans 509 to 30 BCE, officials known as *aediles* maintained the roads the government built. In fact, the *aediles* maintained all public works, including gladiatorial fights and other public games, marketplaces, and roads.

Other Republican officials called *censores*, or censors, had the task of actually creating the roads in the first place. (This was not their only job. The *censores* also kept a census of citizens and property, leased public lands, and awarded contracts to builders of all types.) The censor who built the most famous Roman road—the Via Appia—was

⬡ FLACCUS ON PRIVATE ROADS

Of the surviving ancient Roman writings about Roman roads, among the most important is *De Condicionibus Agrorum*, or *On the Legal Status of Landholdings*. It was penned by a late first-century-CE Roman land surveyor name Siculus Flaccus. In this excerpt, he described private roads that crossed near or over individual rural estates. Flaccus also made the point that local roads, along with other kinds of roads, opened up "communications," or provided a connection between the cities and the countryside.

> There are [road]ways leading across private estates that do not afford passage to everyone, but only to those who need to reach their fields. These ways lead off local roads. Sometimes, too, they fork off from roads belonging jointly to two landowners, who have come to an agreement to take charge of them at the edges of their estates and to share their upkeep. Finally, amongst the public highways, the local roads, and the private ways, those jointly belonging to two landowners all coincide with boundaries. However, these roads were not laid out to act [strictly] as boundaries, but [also] to open up communications.

Siculus Flaccus, *On the Legal Status of Landholdings*, trans. Raymond Chevallier and N.H. Field, in Raymond Chevallier, *Roman Roads*. Berkeley: University of California Press, 1976, pp. 65–66.

Appius Claudius Caecus, who lived in the late 300s and early 200s BCE. He was the also the first Roman road builder (and aqueduct builder) for whom a major public work was named. According to first-century-BCE Roman historian Livy, "The name of Appius has been handed down with more celebrity to posterity, on account of his having made the [famous] road, . . . and for having conveyed water into the city."[10]

The kind of officials who built and repaired the public highways changed in 20 BCE, shortly after the beginning of the period that began in 30 BCE and lasted until 476 CE—the era of the Roman Empire. The first Roman emperor, Augustus Caesar, established the *curatores viarum*. This was a board or council of curators—officials who oversaw public roads in Italy. Usually, a single curator had the responsibility of maintaining and providing security for one major road. Outside of Italy, in Rome's provinces, a provincial governor oversaw all of the roads in his district. He told the public officials under him either to maintain and repair an existing road or to hire contractors to build a new one.

Military, Local, and Private Roads

Flaccus mentioned a second official category of highways—the *viae militares*, which translates as "military roads." As might be expected, they were paid for by the Roman government and constructed by Roman soldiers. Although the military roads were initially built to make it easier and quicker to move armies from one region to another, they swiftly proved handy in other ways. Couriers carrying official mail also came to use them, for example. So did religious pilgrims who felt the urge to visit and worship at well-known shrines far from their homes.

The most common nonmilitary users of these roads, however, were long-distance traders. As Jo-Ann Shelton points out, "Roman traders traveled to every province and shipped goods from Rome to Britain and Syria, from Britain to Greece and Egypt, and from Spain and North Africa to Rome."[11] These enterprising individuals quickly learned that the construction of a new military road had an added bonus. It sometimes opened up new financial opportunities in distant regions that had earlier been too time-consuming, and therefore too expensive, to reach. "Wherever the Roman legions," or armies, went, Shelton continues,

> Roman businessmen followed closely in their wake. And the superb Roman roads built by these legions were used as much for the rapid transport of trade items and business records as for the movement of troops and military supplies. One duty of

Roman garrisons in the provinces was to protect the interests, and lives, of Roman businessmen. And these businessmen seemed to control the economy of many provinces.[12]

Besides public and military roads, Flaccus wrote, there were two other general categories. One consisted of narrower local country roads—in Latin, *actus*—which were located mainly in rural districts called *pagi*. Each *pagus* was made up of one or more villages with a small administrative center run by a local magistrate. "After branching off from the main highway," Flaccus said, "the *actus* go off across the country and often lead to other public ways. They are built and maintained by the *pagi*, that is to say by the magistrates of the *pagi*, who usually see that landowners provide the work force, or rather hand to each landowner the job of looking after the stretch of road going over his land."[13]

Finally, Flaccus explained, there were *privatae*, or roads constructed by private individuals at their own expense. These were situated near or crossed over the rural estates owned by these persons, who were mostly well-to-do. Typically, private roads were narrow, had dirt surfaces, and were not nearly as well built as the larger, government-sponsored roads.

Because these pathways were private, their owners often did not like people trespassing on them. So they sometimes erected signs to warn away intruders. A surviving example reads: "The lower road is the private property of Titus Umbrenius, son of Gaius. Please request permission to use the road. No animal or vehicle traffic allowed."[14]

Differing Road Surfaces

Still another approach to organizing and naming roads was to single out the manner in which Roman builders surfaced them. The type with the hardest and most durable surface—a *via silice strata*, was

A section of Pompeii's once-busy streets provides a quiet place for a modern couple to take a walk. At its height, Pompeii bustled with the comings and goings of merchants, soldiers, peddlers, beggars, and more.

paved with sturdy, resilient stone blocks. Such stone paving replaced dirt surfaces in most of the streets in major Roman cities by the late first century BCE.

A vivid surviving example of such paved city streets can be found in Pompeii. That now-famous Roman city was buried by volcanic ash and pumice in the 79 CE eruption of the volcano Mount Vesuvius, which still overlooks the Bay of Naples on Italy's western coast. The disaster killed several thousand of the city's residents and erased their town from view. However, their misfortune was transformed into fortune for archaeologists and other modern researchers and observers. This is because the volcanic materials that entombed Pompeii also preserved much of it, including its miles of paved streets.

Today those roadways are quiet, says Raymond Chevallier, a noted authority on Roman roads, except for summer tourists who tread on them "under a baking sun." In stark contrast, before the fateful eruption, those streets were alive with activity. Chevallier describes the

> colorful, noisy, swarming crowds of children with their schoolmasters, acrobats, prominent men in sedan chairs or litters with their clients [hangers-on] around them, soldiers, sailors, actors, passing travelers, slaves from distant provinces, well-dressed women on their way to the baths or a show, water-sellers, peddlers, porters [gate- or door-keepers], and horsemen, all adding to the confusion, not to mention beggars and thieves.[15]

Likewise, long stretches of the Via Appia and other key highways that connected the cities featured stone paving. Less solid and durable was the surface of a *via glarea strata*, essentially a gravel road. Finally, the softest and least durable road surface was that of a *via terrena*, or dirt road.

Laying Out a Route

Not surprisingly, a *via terrena* was the easiest and least-complex kind of road to build. In many terrains it required only a few relatively simple steps. The workers first cleared the chosen route of boulders, trees, and other obstacles. Then they flattened and compacted the surface of the roadway. This kind of road clearly required regular upkeep to repair potholes, gullies, and erosion caused by rain, wind, and frequent use. Therefore, on roads or stretches of road where high and/or heavy traffic was expected, it made sense to install a deeper, stronger roadbed with a tougher, more durable surface. This is how major paved roads like the Via Appia came to be built.

Constructing such a major highway was a very time-consuming and costly process. The first task was to choose and lay out the desired route, a job done by *agrimensores*, the ancient Roman equivalent of modern surveyors. Wherever possible, they tried to include

⬡ VARYING ROADBED DEPTHS

In this excerpt from his classic book about travel in the ancient world, the late scholar Lionel Casson explained how the depth of the ditch the Romans dug for a roadbed varied according to the type of terrain and soil in a given area.

> Where the ground was not that resistant, the gangs trenched until they came to a firm enough layer. Into the trench they set the roadbed, usually of more or less rounded stones in a mass of clay or [clay-like] earth. The thickness of the bed depended entirely on how deep the trench had to go. When a raised road was called for, as often happened, the bed was built up until it overtopped the ground level to the desired height. [Sometimes] the surveyors simply could not avoid cutting across marshes or over sand, and then the road gangs had to go to great lengths to prepare a proper bed. One way was to open a deep trench and simply toss in rock until so ponderous a load of stone had been laid down that a firm bed resulted. Where this would not work, they drove in wooden piers, brought in the carpenters to fashion a [horizontal] grillwork of wood, and then laid a gravel road over the wood.

Lionel Casson, *Travel in the Ancient World*. Baltimore: Johns Hopkins University Press, 1994, pp. 169–70.

stretches that were flat and straight because they were the easiest to plan and build. In fact, engineering experts L.A. and J.A. Hamey remark, "Roman roads are particularly famous for their straightness but we must not imagine them as lines ruled on a map. In the first place, the Romans had neither true-to-scale maps nor compasses, and their surveying instruments would be much less accurate than modern theodo-

lites [a precision surveying tool], which depend on the optical lens. We can be sure, however, that the army officers had a remarkable mental grasp of the geography of the areas in which they operated. Roman roads follow very direct routes and run quite straight over considerable distances."[16]

On plains and in open fields, it was fairly easy for Roman surveyors to lay out straight stretches of road using an instrument called a groma. This is an upright stick with two narrow pieces of wood attached to the top, forming a cross. English researcher Adam Hart-Davis explains that a surveyor places a series of poles, flags, or other beacons at intervals in the open area where the road will be and ties strings to each, connecting them. The object is to ensure that the beacons will line up, marking out a straight route, and that is where the groma comes in. The surveyor sticks it in the ground between the first and second beacons. Then, standing behind the groma, Hart-Davis says, "[you] twist it until you can sight along two of the strings to the starting point. Then you walk around the groma and sight the other way, to the second beacon." The person continues to check and re-check the lines of sight "until the strings line up with the start point in one direction and with the second beacon in the other."[17] The surveyor then repeats the process, moving from one beacon to another across the open area.

Invariably, however, the surveyors encountered areas filled with hills, ravines, and/or deep woods. These often blocked their view of what lay ahead, so using normal line-of-sight methods, including the groma, would not work. The exact manner in which Roman surveyors managed to lay out straight routes running through such regions remains somewhat uncertain. One current theory is that they employed fire beacons placed on hilltops. It is possible, the Hameys suggest, "that a line of beacons was used, perhaps by night, but more probably at dawn or dusk. From any beacon it would be possible to see the next in each direction and by some process of laborious adjustment they would be moved into a straight line."[18]

In whatever way the surveyors mapped out a general route with many direct, straight lines in it, their next step was to mark it for the work crews. This was accomplished with wooden stakes. They pounded them into the ground at intervals of a few feet or yards. That showed the workers exactly where to dig.

The Workers

When the surveyors had completed their task, the next step was to prepare the roadbed—the ditch, trench, or furrow into which the actual road materials would be inserted. This step entailed clearing the stake-marked route of trees, rocks, and other obstacles and digging the ditch. Because they had no backhoes, trucks, or other motorized equipment, the Romans had to do these strenuous jobs by hand, sometimes aided by animal power. This meant that hundreds of laborers were needed during the months, and sometimes years, that the road was under construction.

The first Roman roads were initially used mainly by armies on the move. So the road workers were primarily soldiers. As the road network spread farther and farther outward over the years, however, these troops were steadily replaced by civilian workers. A majority of them were free individuals who lived in the towns and regions through which a new road would pass. Some of these laborers were paid in cash. Others took care of part or all of the yearly taxes they owed the government by working on roads or other state-sponsored projects.

Here and there, small numbers of slaves were employed for such work. They usually did the most dangerous tasks, like crawling through underground tunnels that might collapse at any moment. But for most of the work, free persons were usually preferred over slaves. The reason was that, contrary to popular assumptions, in ancient Rome slave labor was not always cheaper than free labor. First, the work done by slaves was not entirely without cost. They had to be fed, clothed, and housed during the long tenure of the project. Also, the Romans had a custom of paying small wages, mostly in the form of periodic tips, to slaves who behaved well and excelled at their work. In addition, on the whole, free laborers who needed the work to feed their families tended to be more reliable than slaves, at least some of whom either had poor work habits or tried to escape.

Surveyors use a groma *(pictured) to lay out straight lines and right angles for roads. Atop a vertical iron staff was a short, pivoting cross arm that supported the main aligning element: a revolving* stelleta *(star). Plumb lines suspended from the ends of the crossed three-foot-long arms allowed surveyors to sight a straight line to markers placed in the ground.*

The Roadbed

Whether they were free or not, once the workers cleared the route of obstacles, they dug the trench for the roadbed. The depth of this ditch depended on the nature of the materials making up the ground in a given area. If the ground was rocky and hard, the trench did not need to be as deep as when the ground was sandy and soft, for instance. On average, the roadbed for a major highway was roughly 4 feet (1.2 m) deep.

Whatever the furrow's depth, it was imperative to fill it with firm materials. That way the road would not sag under the weight of people, animals, wagons, and so forth. So the workers filled in the trench with layers of large and small stones, gravel, bricks, volcanic debris, and/or compressed chalk. In certain situations they first drove in wooden piers (vertical supports), topped them with wooden planks, and then covered the planks with layers of small stones and gravel.

An eyewitness account of the preparation of such a roadbed has survived. It appears in the first-century-CE Roman poet Statius's work the *Silvae*. Describing the creation of a small addition to the Via Appia, he wrote:

> The first task was to prepare the furrow, to open up a track and with deep digging hollow out the earth. The next [step was] to refill the caverned trench and prepare a bed on which the convex surface of the road might be erected, lest the ground should sink or the spiteful earth yield an unstable bed for the deep-set [paving] blocks. . . . What a multitude of hands wrought together at the work! They felled the forests and stripped the hills. Others made smooth the beams and rocks with steel. These bound the stones together and wove fast the work with baked bricks and dingy pumice [volcanic debris].[19]

Surfacing the Roads

When the roadbed was filled in and firm, the final step was to add the surfacing materials. On occasion, stretches of major roads might be surfaced with a layer of hard-packed earth. But more often, gravel or paving stones were preferred because they were more durable and required less frequent repairs. Thus, it was not unusual for a major road like the Via Appia to have alternating sections with surfaces of paving stones, gravel, and compressed earth.

In cases where the surface was to be paved with stones, one approach was to cut them into rectangles. The workers laid them down so that they touched at right angles. Another common method was to cut the blocks into polygons, which had sides of irregular number and shape. These fit together like the pieces of a jigsaw puzzle.

Whatever their shape, these stones, and the roadbeds beneath them, were of such high quality that many sections have survived the ravages of time. Stretches of Roman highway, some of them several miles long, can still be seen in various parts of Europe, Britain, North Africa, and the Middle East. Silent and stalwart, they constitute proof that long ago the phrase "all roads lead to Rome" was not merely an old adage but a living and magnificent reality.

CHAPTER TWO

A Wide Array of Conveniences

The major highways that wind their way across the landscapes of the United States and most other modern countries are not merely barren stretches of tar and concrete. Rather, they frequently feature various services and conveniences. These include rest stops, gas stations, restaurants, motels, convenience stores, and so forth.

The same was true of ancient Rome's primary roads. At intervals, travelers could find inns, all of which served food; stables, some with resident blacksmiths; farm stands that sold fresh fruits and vegetables; chapels where people could stop to pray or simply meditate; and more. Such services and conveniences were, in a sense, small islands of civilization. They made traversing the large tracts of natural wilderness stretching between many of the towns more bearable.

Built-In Road Features

Also like their modern counterparts, some of the conveniences along the Roman highways were built into the roads themselves. For example, paved Roman roads curved upward slightly in the middle and tapered gradually toward the sides. Called cambering, this kept rainwater from pooling on the road. The water drained away into ditches that workers had dug along the roadsides.

Another built-in, very convenient road feature consisted of artificial ruts carved into the surfaces of the paving stones. Their purpose was to act as guides for the wheels of wagons and chariots and thereby prevent them from sliding and skidding. Likewise, the road builders laid out knee-high, flattened stones along the roadsides every few hundred feet or so. This service was for travelers with horses. Stirrups, which modern riders use to mount their steeds, had not yet been invented. So the flat-topped stones acted as boosters, making it easier for dismounted Roman riders to climb back onto their horses.

Still another aid to travelers on Rome's roads were *miliaria*, or milestones, modern versions of which are visible along today's highways. Roman milestones were set up at varying intervals, most often a Roman mile, which was a bit shorter than a modern mile. A typical *miliarium* was made of limestone, granite, or sandstone; cylinder shaped; about 10 feet (3 m) high; and roughly 2 feet (61 cm) wide. About eight thousand Roman milestones have survived—among them some twenty-three hundred in North Africa; six hundred each in Italy, France, and Germany; and almost one hundred in Britain.

Carved into these stones were the distances between towns and cities along the road. Also, some of the markers mentioned the name of the person who had built the road. If he was an emperor, the inscription could be quite long and involved, as in the case of one marker dating from about 354 CE in what is now Serbia. It praises the emperor Constantius (reigned 353–361), lists his illustrious forbears, and calls him a "very great and noble first citizen," a "very great pontiff," and the "father of his country."[20] It also praises him for building roads, renovating bridges, and erecting milestones in the province of Illyria (now Serbia).

Posting Stations and Couriers

These conveniences were there for all who used the Roman roads. But there were several other services and amenities along the roads that at least at first were intended for use by specific individuals. This

An ancient Roman milestone, still standing along an old road in Italy, told travelers how much further they had to go before reaching the next town or city. Such milestones were usually made from limestone, granite, or sandstone.

included the *mutationes*, or posting stations. They were initially created for members of the *cursus publicus*, or government post, a system of messengers employed by government officials.

During the early Republic, official messages were relatively few and went out on an irregular basis. Over time, however, as Rome's realm expanded, the number of messages, as well as messengers, increased. For a long time those couriers were mainly slaves and freedmen (slaves who had been freed by their owners).

At the dawn of the Empire, this system changed in a big way as the first emperor, Augustus, set up the larger and more regular *cursus publicus*. Its couriers were most often soldiers. Although they sometimes rode horses, most often the Roman messengers used horse-drawn wagons. Archaeologists found a carving of such a wagon, called a *reda*, on the gravestone of one of those messengers. It has four wheels and is pulled by three horses. Urging them on with his whip is a driver perched in the front of the cart. As described by the late, noted historian Lionel Casson, behind the driver sat "the courier, wearing a hooded traveling cloak and holding what seems to be a riding crop. Behind him, facing rearward, is his servant, who sits on the baggage and clutches a lance with a distinctive head, a special insignia of office showing that his master was attached to the staff of the local governor."[21]

On average, messengers like the one pictured on the grave marker traveled around 45 miles (72 km) a day. If the mission was urgent, however, they could go close to three times that distance per day. Clearly, they required lodging and food during their journeys, and the posting stations built along the main roads fulfilled that need. Such a station provided fresh horses, as well as a new wheel if one was needed. The facility also had drinking water and basic foodstuffs for the horses and men.

The imperial Roman government relied heavily on its official messages getting through as fast as possible. This explains why it built *mutationes* at regular intervals along the major roads. Evidence unearthed by archaeologists shows that there was a station at an average interval of only 9,500 paces. A Roman pace was the distance between an adult male's outstretched hands, or about 5 feet (1.5 m). So the average distance between posting stations was 47,520 feet (14,484 m), or 9 miles (14.5 km).

Inns Along the Way

In addition to these stations, which offered only basic services, the main roads were dotted with larger inns, known as *mansiones*. Another Latin word that was sometimes used to denote an inn was *taberna* (from which the modern word *tavern* comes). More often, though, a *taberna* described a bar that sold wine, beer, and/or fast food.

The inns were located at fairly regular intervals of 20 to 30 miles (32 to 48 km). They served any and all travelers, along with some couriers. Inns featured the same facilities as posting stations but were generally more spacious and comfortable, as well as better equipped. They also had the means to put up a number of people for the night. Also, inns were privately built and owned, rather than run by the government like the *mutationes*. (Still, the inns' owners were obligated by law to allow official couriers to stay for free.)

The names of Roman inns were typically colorful. Most bore the names of gods; The Mercury and Apollo and The Diana were widely popular. A sign located at the entrance to The Mercury and Apollo in what is now Lyons, France, has survived. It is particularly noteworthy because it mentions the innkeeper's name—Septumanus. The sign reads: "Mercury promises gain, Apollo health, Septumanus hospitality. Whoever enters here will be the better. Therefore, stranger, watch where you lodge."[22]

Lodgings and Meals

Other inns were often named for everyday tools, weapons, foods, and other objects. Among them were The Wheel, The Olives, The Sword, and The Skull Cap. Also common were animal names such as The Serpent, The Elephant, The Little Eagle, The Rooster, and The Camel.

However they were named, all inns offered lodging, food, fresh pack animals, wagon wheels, and other travelers' needs. Historians know how the typical inn was laid out because several of these facilities have been excavated. One found in what is now Austria was two stories high, 70 feet (21 m) long, and 40 feet (12 m) wide. It featured a large kitchen and dining room on the ground floor and several small bedchambers on the upper floor. Some of the rooms were heated in the winter, thanks to hollow spaces beneath the floor. These connected to a wood-burning, kiln-like furnace situated just outside the structure.

The inn also had a blacksmith's shop, a shed for wagons, and a stable big enough to keep about a dozen horses or other animals.

In some areas, especially where a major road passed through or near a town, travelers had a choice of eating places. If they did not wish to have their meals in an inn, they could go to a restaurant. All towns had small snack bars (*thermopolia*) that sold both hot and cold fast food. Common fare included meat, bean, or lentil stews; fish; porridge; bread; cheese; fruit; and baked pastries for desert. Pompeii, a typical large Roman town, had close to two hundred such snack bars. There were also more formal sit-down restaurants (*popinae*), often with two or three small dining rooms. Pompeii's main street alone had twenty eating places of one kind or another.

⬡ TURN AT THE FIG TREE

Even with guidebooks, it was not always easy to find one's way within the Roman road system. This was particularly true in Rome and other large cities, which contained vast jumbles of small streets, many of which had no signs or names. This could make giving directions long-winded and confusing. An example appears in *The Brothers*, a comedy by the Roman playwright Terence. In this passage, a slave is trying to tell one of the brothers where to find the other brother's house.

(pointing) Go right up that street. When you come there, there is a descent right opposite that goes downward. Go straight down that. Afterward, on this side (indicating with one hand), there is a chapel. Close by it is a narrow lane where there's also a great wild fig tree. . . . You know the house of Cratinus, the rich man? When you have passed it, keep straight along that street on the left hand. Before you come to the city gate, just by that pond, there is a baker's shop and opposite to it a joiner's. He [your brother] is there.

Terence, *The Brothers*, in *The Comedies of Terence*, trans. Henry T. Riley. Charleston, SC: BiblioBazaar, 2010, p. 230.

Whether or not a highway passed through a town, travelers who could not afford or did not desire to stay at an inn and/or eat at a restaurant sometimes had another choice. Lodgings in private homes were available here and there, just as they are in many countries today. The rooms in such guesthouses were usually cheaper than those at the inns. The hosts often included their prices, along with other information, on the signs they put up to lure travelers. One guesthouse that has been excavated had a plaque hanging on an outer wall that revealed its owner's sense of humor. "If you are clean and neat," it says, "you'll find a room waiting for you here. If you're a slob, well, I blush to say it, but you're welcome as well!"[23]

Forms of Transportation

No evidence has yet been found to show that imperial couriers used private guesthouses while on the job. But it is possible that a few professional messengers may have gotten to know the owners of such places over the years and stayed with them when time permitted. Meanwhile, there were certainly plenty of other customers for those owners to choose from. Besides the couriers, among the biggest users of lodgings and other facilities along the roads were merchants and traders. If someone could go back and witness Roman society firsthand, classical scholar Philip Matyszak says, he or she would see that "businessmen and merchants are constantly on the move," some selling all manner of everyday products, while a few transport "cages of exotic animals, either for display or death in the insatiable Roman circuses. There are local traders, following a circuit of towns according to the pattern of the markets. Most rural towns do not have shops, but hold markets at regular intervals."[24]

Others who used the inns, snack bars, and guesthouses included all sorts of noncommercial travelers, from soldiers going home on leave, to sightseers, to ordinary folk visiting relatives or friends who lived in distant towns. Whatever their reasons for using the highways, all of these travelers had something important in common: They were obliged to employ the few forms of transportation that then existed.

Besides walking, one of the more common ways one traveled on the roads was to ride a donkey, mule (a cross between a donkey and a horse), or horse. Horses were not ridden by average travelers very often, largely because they were more expensive to raise and feed than donkeys or mules. Most horses were used by soldiers, couriers, or well-to-do individuals. When the choice was between a donkey and a mule, most people picked the latter, partly because a mule is stronger than a donkey. A mule can carry up to 450 pounds (204 kg), compared to a donkey's maximum load of about 250 pounds (113 kg).

Wagons were also widely employed for travel. (One important exception to their use was when part of the journey occurred on secondary roads that were too narrow for wagons. In that case mules or donkeys were preferred.) During the Empire, Roman passenger wagons featured a light and flexible main frame most often made of wickerwork or thin strips of wood. The wheels had spokes that connected the central hub to a "tire" composed of a wooden rim covered with a single, thin strip of iron. The animals that pulled these wagons included donkeys, mules, horses, and—for very large wagons with unusually heavy loads—oxen.

Rich Romans could afford to travel in luxury. They lounged in litters, traveling couches that featured soft pillows and canopies with curtains for privacy. If the trip was fairly short, four to eight slaves lugged the litter, bearing the supporting bars on their shoulders. For longer trips, it was common to rest the bars on the backs of donkeys or mules.

The Appropriate Baggage

Whether they were wealthy or of average means, travelers on the roads knew they had to carry suitable supplies for the trip. First, they needed to dress appropriately. The most obvious example was wearing lighter clothing in the summer and heavier, warmer garments in the winter.

There was also the question of how many outfits to bring on the

THE THREAT OF ROBBERY

Among the ever-present dangers along Rome's roads was the threat of robbery. Particularly on lonely stretches of highway far from cities and towns, thieves sometimes laid in wait for unwary travelers. An example of highway robbery on a Roman road was captured in *The Golden Ass*, a novel by the second-century-CE Roman writer Apuleius. "What a mess I'm in!" the victim exclaims as he begins to describe his regrettable experience.

> I have fallen into this misfortune through seeking a diversion at a celebrated gladiatorial show. You will remember that I made for Macedonia on a business trip. I was busy there for nine months and more, and was making my way home with a good bit of money in my pocket. Shortly before reaching Larissa [in Greece], where I intended to take in the show as I was passing through, I was making my way along a trackless, pitted valley when I was held up by some brigands of massive physique who robbed me of all my money. When I finally got away, I stopped at an inn because I was badly shaken up.

Apuleius, *The Golden Ass*, trans. P.G. Walsh. Oxford: Oxford University Press, 1994, p. 5.

journey. Because they walked or rode donkeys or wagons, ancient travelers plodded along at a pace that people today would view as unbelievably slow. Moderately long trips along Rome's roads took at least several days, and journeys lasting weeks or even a few months were not unusual. So the average Roman traveler had to carry enough clothes to last a while. Also, it was important to bring along certain special items, such as shoes that could stand up to heavy wear, a broad-rimmed hat to shade one's head on sunny days, and a long cape to protect against wind and/or cold.

In general, the amount of baggage travelers carried depended in large part on their financial means. Poorer folk, who made up the bulk of the Roman realm's population, could not afford to stay at inns every night. So when the weather permitted, they camped outside, sleeping in bedrolls or small tents. These naturally added to the weight of the baggage. Some people also brought along cooking pots, plates, cups, eating utensils, and other items for consuming makeshift meals. In addition, they kept their money, jewelry, or other valuables in a bag that hung from their waist. Hoping to keep those articles secure against robbers, many travelers carried a knife, sword, or other weapon as well.

Another type of item often carried by travelers on the roads was something to be delivered to someone either during or at the end of the journey. One common example was a gift for the person or institution (such as a temple or shrine) they intended to visit. Travelers might also bring along smaller gifts for the owners of guesthouses where they planned to stay during the trip.

One more kind of delivered item was personal letters. Some were written by friends or acquaintances, although it was just as common for travelers to carry letters for persons they did not know. This was because the couriers of the government post carried only official mail, and no public postal system like those taken for granted across the modern world then existed. Wealthy Romans could afford to hire their own couriers, but average people could not. So they had no choice but to rely on travelers to relay their letters for them. The most common practice was to wait at a major road crossing and find someone who was headed to the town or region where the letter's recipient lived. Most people were happy to perform this service because they wanted it to be available to them, too, when they needed it.

Guide Books

Still another common article carried by voyagers on the Roman roads was a map or guide book, conveniences that continue to be widely used today. No less than modern drivers, travelers on Rome's roads frequently needed decent directions to find their way over long distances. They also wanted to be able to find the locations of the many inns, guesthouses, eating spots, and other facilities that catered to travelers.

The solution was to purchase pamphlet-like road guides known as *itineraria* (the derivation of the modern word *itinerary*). A typical guide showed the locations of cities, towns, inns, religious shrines, and other prominent places that existed along a given road. A handful of these guides have survived, including one dating to the early 300s CE. At the time, Christianity was rapidly growing in popularity across the Empire, and this particular itinerary was aimed directly at Christians who desired to go on pilgrimages to shrines in various parts of the realm.

The book displays the major roads running from Burdigala (modern Bordeaux), in what is now France, to Jerusalem, in what is now Israel. The latter was already becoming known as the Holy Land because it was the region where Jesus had lived and preached and where many of the stories in the Old Testament had supposedly taken place. The section of the book that shows France includes roads totaling some 370 miles (595 km) and lists eleven inns and thirty posting stations. Shown in addition are a number of short side trips. Historians think these were the routes that then led to local Christian churches and/or guesthouses that were run by or catered to Christians.

Maps

There were also Roman maps that exhibited many of the same roadside stops shown in the road guides. A now famous surviving example, measuring 13 inches (33 cm) wide by 22 feet (6.7 m) long, is known as the *Tabula Peutingeriana*, or Peutinger Table. Found in Germany in the late fifteenth century, it was an earlier medieval copy of an ancient Roman map. It is presently on display in a museum in Vienna, Austria.

The Peutinger Table shows the Roman Empire's provinces and the major roads passing through each. It not only lists the towns and cities, but also displays little numbers that tell the distance from one city to another in Roman miles. Various symbols, or icons, mark inns,

A map known as the Peutinger Table depicts the Roman Empire's provinces and major roads and includes icons that mark inns and other places of interest along the roads. Shown here is a section of the part of the map depicting what is now France.

posting stations, and other travelers' facilities along the roads. These icons provided information about the quality of these places in the same manner that many modern maps and guidebooks do. Casson described some of these icons in the Peutinger Table. A "picture of a four-sided building with a courtyard in the center," he said,

> stands for a town or country inn of some consequence, one that could offer a considerable range of services. A picture of the front of a house with a twin-peaked roof stands for a less pretentious country inn. Twin cupolas instead of peaks means the same grade of inn but with ample water available. A single-peaked, boxlike cottage stands for a very modest inn.

Names with no picture alongside probably indicate the simplest form of hostel, places that could furnish little more than water, shelter, a bare meal, and a fresh relay of animals.[25]

Unifying the Realm

A comfortable trip was never guaranteed, even for the best-equipped and informed travelers. No matter the traveler's social status or luck with weather, Roman roads could be uncomfortable and the travel grueling. Historians know this because written descriptions of such trips have survived.

The most famous example was penned by the widely admired first-century-BCE Roman poet Quintus Horatius Flaccus, popularly known as Horace. He described an outing he took on the Via Appia from Rome to Brundisium, a distance of 370 miles (595 km), which took several days to complete. In his narrative, Horace complained about a hot, windy mountain road, polluted water that upset his stomach, mosquitoes and croaking frogs that disrupted his sleep, and greedy innkeepers who overcharged him and his traveling companions. Only part way through the trek, Horace grumbled, "we were exhausted" and the expedition "was made even more uncomfortable by rain."[26]

In spite of unhappy journeys like the one Horace recalled, the Roman road system was one of the marvels of the ancient world. On the one hand, it was a first-class engineering feat. On the other, it carried Roman life and customs far and wide, thereby unifying the diverse lands and peoples of Europe, North Africa, and much of the Middle East.

Furthermore, Rome's roads strongly influenced the futures of these places long after the Roman realm ceased to exist. Many of the inns and other roadside conveniences developed into villages and then into towns over time. As Raymond Chevallier says, "The initial grouping of population centered on the road was followed by a second phase in which there grew up a system of scattered settlements linked by short antennae to the main road."[27] In this way many of the best-known cities and towns in modern Europe can trace their beginnings to once solitary yet vital stops on the world's first great road network.

CHAPTER THREE

Providing Life-Giving Water

Next to Rome's road system, few ancient structures were as large and impressive as its network of aqueducts. These artificial waterways, which took the form of stone channels, transferred immense quantities of water to Rome and the realm's other major cities and towns. Like the roads, which made travel and trade easier, the aqueducts were an example of the use of engineering to significantly improve the basic standard of living for millions of citizens. As Jo-Ann Shelton points out:

> People need a constant supply of fresh water, but in a city it is difficult for each person to be responsible for finding and maintaining his own water supply. The Romans solved this problem by building an amazing system of aqueducts which carried water to their cities from areas many miles away. Since the lives of the residents depended on this water supply, it was essential that the aqueducts be kept in good repair and that the water flow freely. The aqueducts were so well instructed and maintained that many are still standing today.[28]

Ingenuity, Boldness, and Pride

Despite the enormity and the success of this mighty water delivery system, the Romans did not invent the idea of aqueducts any more than they did the concept of roads. In the late eighth or early seventh century BCE, when Rome was still a dirty little town with no empire, a local king in faraway Mesopotamia (what is now Iraq) erected an imposing stone aqueduct to transport water from a canal to the city of Nineveh. Roughly a century later, a Greek ruler built an aqueduct on the Aegean island of Samos. It ran through the center of a small mountain for more than half a mile.

Impressive as they were in their own time, however, these efforts paled in comparison to those of ancient Rome. What the Romans lacked in originality, they abundantly made up for in ingenuity, boldness, and sheer determination. When they finally set their sights on creating aqueducts, they easily outdid all who had come before. The Roman Empire's capital eventually boasted eleven large-scale aqueducts that together stretched an incredible 260 miles (418 km). Moreover, hundreds of other similar water channels were constructed in Italy, Spain, Greece, North Africa, and elsewhere in the Empire.

Hundreds of miles of these structures remain intact or largely so today. This allows experts to study them firsthand and determine how they were built and the way they operated. But this is not the only reason that archaeologists and historians know a great deal about Rome's aqueducts. There is also the fortunate fact that an entire book written by an ancient Roman water commissioner has survived. That individual was Sextus Julius Frontinus, appointed to his post by the emperor Nerva in 97 CE. An honest, hardworking public official, Frontinus was also a productive and talented writer. In considerable detail, he described most of what he knew about Rome's complex water system in the appropriately titled book *The Aqueducts of Rome*.

WORDS IN CONTEXT
cistern
A device that captures and stores rainwater.

Frontinus was not only very knowledgeable about the aqueducts but also extremely proud of them. Like most Romans, he believed that Roman civilization was superior in many ways to that of other peoples—a supremacy he believed was proved by the vast accomplishments of Roman engineering. "With such an array of indispens-

An aqueduct dating from the time of ancient Rome can still be seen in Spain. The Romans erected aqueducts for carrying fresh water throughout the empire.

able structures carrying so many waters," he bragged about Rome's aqueducts, "compare, if you will, the idle [Egyptian] Pyramids or the useless, though famous, works of the Greeks!"[29]

From Springs and Wells to Aqueducts

One reason that Frontinus's book about the aqueducts is so valuable is that he covered the subject in a very logical, systematic, and clear-cut manner. In so doing, he provided much information about Roman life and customs both before and after the water system was created. For example, he explained that in the centuries prior to erecting the aqueducts, the Romans got the water they needed for drinking, bathing, and cooking from rivers, springs, and wells.

Archaeologists have confirmed that these natural sources were supplemented by cisterns. A cistern is a collection device for capturing and storing rainwater. The early Romans most often put them on rooftops, but ground-level versions later became common, especially the *compluvium/impluvium* arrangement. This was seen most commonly in a house's entrance hall or some other central corridor or lobby. The *compluvium* was a rectangular opening in the roof, and

 FRONTINUS'S BOOK ON WATER SYSTEMS

The book that Sextus Julius Frontinus penned about Rome's aqueducts is filled with information about how the aqueducts and the complex water distribution systems on their front ends worked; how the aqueducts were maintained; and the daily output of each of these important water channels. In the introduction to the book, Frontinus told how he approached the writing. "I have gathered in this sketch," he said, as many scattered facts "as I have been able to get together." The book "will serve especially for my own instruction and guidance, being prepared, as it is, at the beginning of my administration." Then he explained the nature of the information he intended to talk about, saying he would first name the various aqueducts entering the capital city. And then,

> I will tell by whom, under what consuls, and in what year after the founding of the city each one was brought in; then at what point and at what milestone each water was taken, how far each is carried in a subterranean channel, how far on substructures, how far on arches. Then I will give the elevation of each [and] how many public reservoirs there are, and from these how much [water] is delivered to public works, how much to ornamental fountains [and so forth].

Sextus Julius Frontinus, *The Aqueducts of Rome*, in *The Stratagems and the Aqueducts of Rome*, trans. C.E. Bennett. Cambridge, MA: Harvard University Press, 1993, pp. 331, 333, 335.

the *impluvium* a shallow basin situated directly below it. Rainwater flowed across the roof (which was tilted a bit toward the middle), through the opening, and down into the basin.

Such natural sources of water continued to be exploited by some people well after the first aqueducts were built, Frontinus said. In part, this was because the Romans were sentimental, and they admired, indeed at times even revered, tradition. They had much "esteem for springs," Frontinus wrote, and viewed them with veneration and great respect. "They are believed to bring healing to the sick."[30]

Nevertheless, drawing water from the springs by hand was a laborious and time-consuming process. It worked well enough for a small number of people living in a village. But in larger towns, and particularly in full-fledged cities like Rome, this method was no longer practical. It was "insufficient," Frontinus said, "to meet both the public needs and the luxurious private demands of the day."[31] As urban populations swelled into the tens of thousands and then into the hundreds of thousands, the demand for plentiful amounts of fresh water rapidly grew. So building aqueducts became the only logical solution to the problem.

The first aqueduct serving the city of Rome, the Aqua Appia, was erected in 312 BCE. It was named for Appius Claudius, the same public official who constructed the first major road, the Via Appia. Frontinus's book provides a detailed account of how the Aqua Appia came to be, as well as its physical size and characteristics. Frontinus described the channel's length as 11,190 paces, which in modern terms translates to 10.5 miles (16.9 km). He also noted that some of the water was carried aboveground on stone supports that rose 60 paces, or 300 feet (91 m), in the air.

Finding Pure Water

Aqueducts like the Aqua Appia carried water from a rural source to an urban center. So the first step in building such a structure was to locate a plentiful and reliable water source. Sometimes this was a fairly simple task. For instance, the countryside near the city of Rome had many rolling hills and small mountains. Water from rain and melting snow flowed downward from these places, some of it feeding into local rivers. The remaining outflow sank down into the ground and later bubbled up here and there as freshwater springs. Roman engineers rightly concluded that if these springs were properly tapped, they could provide Rome with the large amounts of water its inhabitants required.

In contrast, freshwater springs were far fewer or situated considerably deeper, in drier, less hilly regions. So finding water for a city was not always as straightforward as it was in the case of the Roman capital. As time went on, the Romans found ways of locating water that was not plainly visible at ground level.

Historians and other modern observers know about these ancient methods of finding water thanks to Marcus Vitruvius Pollio, popularly known simply as Vitruvius. He was a Roman architect who was prominent from roughly 46 to 30 BCE. Not long after he retired, he wrote a long thesis titled *On Architecture*, which has survived complete. The book covers numerous aspects of Roman engineering, including those relating to water sources. To seek out hard-to-find underground sources, Vitruvius said, one should "fall on one's face before sunrise in the place where the search is to take place, and placing and supporting one's chin on the ground, to look round the neighborhood." Moreover, he added, "digging is to be carried out where moisture seems to curl upwards and rise into the air, for this indication cannot arise on dry ground."[32]

Another way to locate fresh water, Vitruvius stated, was to closely observe the plants in a given area. Certain kinds of plants "grow in marshy places," he said, "for these, settling below the level of the rest of the ground, receive water from the rains and from the rest of the land in winter, and because of their capacity to retain moisture." If water was discovered this way, Vitruvius asserted, the person should

WORDS IN CONTEXT

specus
The water channel lying at the heart of a Roman aqueduct.

follow a set procedure: "A hole is to be dug not less than three feet square and five feet deep, and about sunset a bronze or lead vessel, or a basin, is to be placed there." The next day, that container should "be opened, and if there are drops of water and moisture in the vessel, water will be found."[33]

Discovering a water source was one thing, Vitruvius went on, and finding one that was pure enough for people to drink was quite another. The realization that some sources were impure is what made the Romans of his day avoid river water whenever possible, as it was usually full of sediments. The chemical treatments used to purify water today were unknown to the Romans, of course. So they developed their own methods of testing for purity. If a water sample was clear looking and did not cause a person to develop "inflamed eyes," Vitruvius wrote, "the water will pass. If a fresh spring be dug, and the water, being sprinkled over a vessel of Corinthian [copper or gold] or any other good bronze, leave no trace [of residue], the water is very good. Or if water is boiled in a copper vessel and is allowed to stand and then poured off, it will also pass the test if no sand or mud is found in the bottom of the copper vessel."[34]

Laying Out the Route

Once a plentiful, safe source of water had been found, the engineers and surveyors could begin planning and laying out the aqueduct. The initial stages of the project were the most difficult and time-consuming. This was because surveying the land for an aqueduct was very different from doing so for a road. In the case of the latter, the object was to create a route that was as straight and direct as possible. In contrast, aqueducts required frequent twists and turns.

The reason for this zigzag approach was that a Roman aqueduct transported water by taking advantage of the natural force of gravity. The *specus*, Latin for the water channel that constituted an aqueduct, slanted very slightly downward from a horizontal position. The degree of incline was just enough to cause the water to flow downward and away from its source. The exact amount of this slant

BLUNDERS IN A TUNNEL

When necessary, Roman builders tunneled right through small mountains to avoid routing an aqueduct all the way around such obstacles. They dug two shafts from opposite sides of a hill at the same time, hoping they would meet in the right spot in the center. This proved to be extremely tricky with very long tunnels. This very situation occurred in 152 CE while two teams of Roman workers dug the opposing ends of a tunnel for an aqueduct located in what is now Algeria, in North Africa. The teams missed each other by several feet, prompting the irate engineer in charge of the project to write:

> As always happens in these cases, the fault was attributed to me, the engineer, as though I had not taken all precautions to ensure the success of the work. What could I have done better? For I began by surveying and taking the levels of the mountain, I drew plans and sections of the whole work, to take extra precaution, I summoned the contractor and his workmen and began the excavation in their presence. . . . [Later, I found that] the contractor and his assistants had made blunder upon blunder. In each section of the tunnel they had diverged from the strait line, each towards the right.

Quoted in Ivor B. Hart, *The Great Engineers*. Freeport, NY: Books for the Libraries, 1967, p. 4.

varied a bit from one area to another, but on average it was approximately 2 to 3 feet (61 to 91 cm) per mile. This means that the water moved through the aqueduct because the point at which the water started was a little higher than the desired destination.

The upshot of these widely recognized facts was that the planners laid out the *specus* so that it maintained the desired slant no matter how many times it was necessary to change its direction. The number of changes depended on the lay of the land, which varied from one place to another. As a result, a typical aqueduct tended to meander through the countryside in its own unique fashion. According to

French architectural historian Jean-Pierre Adam, "Obstacles had to be crossed or bypassed without imposing too many constraints on the average incline to be maintained. In fact, it was preferable to avoid level stretches, which caused the water to stagnate, but equally too strong [steep] an incline brought about the rapid erosion of the watertight lining of the channel."[35] Thus, the engineers and builders had to be careful to ensure that the water channel was tipped at just the right angle everywhere along the route, a task that required a lot of skill and attention to detail.

Excavating the Trench and Tunnels

With the water channel's route mapped out, the head builder stepped in with his crews of laborers. As happened when building a road, their initial task was to clear the route of boulders, trees, and any other obstacles. Then they started digging a trench in which to lay the *specus*.

Some of these workers, like most members of the road gangs, were free individuals who dwelled in the towns along the aqueduct's course. For the sections of the structure that directly approached an urban center, many of the workers were unemployed free residents of that city. Happy for some gainful employment, even if temporary, they walked or rode out to the construction site each day until the project was finished.

As was the case with all kinds of Roman menial work, however, the more grueling and hazardous jobs were done by slaves. The common reasoning was that the death of a slave on the job was less of a loss to society than that of a free person. Typical of these dangerous tasks was creating and working in narrow, vertical shafts. Sometimes, instead of digging an ordinary horizontal tunnel through a hillside, the builders called for sinking vertical shafts at intervals along the hillside. Slaves then climbed down into the cramped darkness and dug a tunnel in which to place the *specus* by laboriously connecting the bottoms of the shafts. Other such shafts were installed for inspection, cleaning, and repairs of the *specus*. These inspection shafts were spaced at intervals of 233 feet (71 m). L.A. and

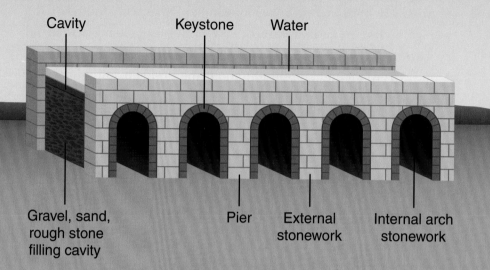

Parts of an Aqueduct

Cavity

Keystone

Water

Gravel, sand, rough stone filling cavity

Pier

External stonework

Internal arch stonework

Source: V. Ryan, "Roman Bridge and Aqueduct Construction," 2009. www.technologystudent.com.

J.A. Hamey comment that those who dug them were unfortunate indeed, for "without free-flowing air, the atmosphere" inside the shafts and tunnels "would soon become foul from the oil-lamps and the breathing of the workmen."[36]

Whether the diggers were free or not, they all agreed that it was easier to excavate the aqueduct's main trench in places where the ground was soft and shovels could be used. In contrast, rockier areas required a lot of smashing with picks and hammers and prying with levers. As the ditch got progressively deeper, the workers inserted sturdy lengths of timber to shore up the dirt along the sides in preparation for laying down the blocks of stone that would make up the channel.

All during this stage of the work, it was crucial to ensure that the bottom, or floor, of the trench maintained the desired incline so that the water would flow properly through the channel. So an on-site engineer or surveyor periodically took careful measurements of the trench. If the degree of slant was incorrect, he ordered the workmen to make the necessary alterations.

Buried and Unburied

When those in charge determined that the incline was right, it was time to construct the *specus* within the excavated trench. This conduit, composed of heavy stone blocks measuring on average 20 by 50 inches (51 by 127 cm), was almost as wide and tall as an average modern doorway. Because it would carry water that people would drink, it was important to keep its interior surfaces as clean as possible. So a gang of workers coated the inside with a special mortar that kept dirt particles from entering through the cracks between the stone blocks.

When this sealing layer of mortar was dry in the section of the channel at hand, the foreman gave the order to lay down the stone blocks that made up the ceiling of the conduit. After that, the workers shoveled the excavated dirt back into the trench, burying the *specus*. If the ground above the channel and the positions of the inspection shafts were left unmarked, in theory their exact locations could be lost over time. So the workers set up special aqueduct marker stones, called *cippi*, along the route. (During the first two centuries in which the Romans built aqueducts, enemy armies continued to threaten Italy and even Rome itself now and then. So the locations of the buried aqueducts were purposely left unmarked during this time. That way, no invader would be able to find and destroy the capital's precious water supply.)

WORDS IN CONTEXT

cippi
Stone markers that showed the location of the buried portions of Rome's aqueducts.

Once the *cippi* were in place, the only sections of an aqueduct that remained unburied were those that ran for short stretches across gullies, valleys, and downward-sloping plains. These portions of the water channel were carried atop stone bridges or arcades—a kind of bridge held up by a series of graceful arches. However, most of a *specus* was located underground. For instance, of the 260 miles (418 km) constituting the combined length of Rome's eleven aqueducts, the portions featuring arcades and bridges ran for only 30 miles (48 km), or about one-ninth of the total distance.

Constructing the Arches

The arches that made up an arcade have long been seen as a Roman trademark. (The Romans did not invent the arch. But they used it so often and in such impressive ways that it became forever associated with them.) Each arch rested atop two vertical stone supports called piers. The arch itself was composed of two curved lines, or arcs, of wedge-shaped stones that met at a central stone (called the keystone) at the top.

To keep the wedges from falling while the arch was under construction, the builders employed a temporary support. Known as centering, it was a wooden framework shaped to fit snugly into the semicircular space directly below the arch. Thus, the centering held up the stone wedges until the keystone was inserted. After the centering was removed, the weight of the stones that made up the arch was displaced through its curve and passed on to the piers, which in turn transferred it into the ground.

WORDS IN CONTEXT

centering
A wooden framework that temporarily supported an arch's curved stones while the arch was under construction.

In the sections of an aqueduct that used arcades, a single row of arches was usually enough to carry the *specus* at the desired height above the ground, river, or whatever type of terrain was involved. On occasion, however, more height was required. To meet this need, the builders added one or more additional arcades atop the initial one. An example of a two-tier Roman aqueduct arcade has survived at Segovia, in north-central Spain. It was so well built and remains in such good condition that the water channel it supports is still in use. Each and every day it provides the town's residents with fresh water from a stream 11 miles (17.7 km) away.

Probably the most famous of all the surviving multiple aqueduct arcades erected by the Romans crosses over a deep valley near Nimes, in southern France. Called the Pont du Gard, it features an impressive three-tiered stack of arcades. Moreover, this magnificent structure carried not only an aqueduct, but also two paved roads. These ran along the first and second arcades, which are 20 and 15 feet (6 and 4.6 m) wide respectively. The narrower third and topmost arcade, meanwhile, carried a portion of an aqueduct that stretched for a total of 31 miles (50 km). Today towering engineering works like the Pont du Gard provide tangible proof that Frontinus was right when he said of Rome's aqueducts, "they are structures of the greatest magnitude."[37]

CHAPTER FOUR

Flowing from Fountains and Faucets

"Let us now move on to achievements which are unsurpassed because of their real value," the elder Pliny wrote in the 70s CE. "The most recent and costly project, begun by the emperor Gaius and completed by Claudius, has surpassed all previous aqueducts." The structure to which Pliny referred was the Aqua Claudia. It had been initiated in the reign of the third emperor, Gaius Caesar (more commonly called Caligula), in 38 CE and completed by his successor, Claudius, in 52 CE. During the building of the aqueduct, Pliny continued, "the springs called Curtius and Caeruleus, as well as the Anio Novus [aqueduct], were made to flow into Rome from the fortieth milestone at such a high level as to provide water for all the hills of the city."[38]

The Aqua Claudia was the ninth aqueduct erected to supply the Empire's capital city. Today it is the best preserved of the eleven water channels that eventually flowed into Rome. Pliny also wrote about the longest of the eleven—the Aqua Marcia, at 58.4 miles (94 km), finished in 144 BCE. "The top prize for cool, wholesome water," he said, went to "the Aqua Marcia, a gift, among others, of the gods to our city."[39]

Together, the nine local aqueducts that Pliny knew delivered upward of 200 million gallons (757 million L) of freshwater to Rome each day. (That amount rose to an estimated 250 million gallons, or 946 million liters, per day by the early 200s, after the addition of two more aqueducts.) During Pliny's era, the city of Rome had about 1 million residents. So the aqueducts generated some 200 gallons (757 L) of water per person per day. (By contrast, the water department of the average American town supplies only about 125 gallons, or 473 liters, per person per day.)

This huge quantity of water entering ancient Rome each day mostly originated at springs in the nearby mountains. Together, those springs and the stone channels that carried the water across the countryside constituted what was in a sense the aqueducts' backside. When the water reached Rome, it entered the water system's front. That front consisted of a complex distribution network that included reservoirs, settling tanks, water pipes, fountains, public and private baths, faucets, and so forth. As *curator aquarum*, or director of Rome's water commission, Frontinus was as much in charge of the system's front as he was its backside.

Cleaning the Incoming Water

The first and most crucial area the incoming water entered when it reached the city was the *castellum aquae*. Translating literally as "water fortress," it was the water system's main distribution center. Not only in Rome, but also in any urban center with an aqueduct, the *castellum aquae* was situated on an outer edge of town and at the highest elevation possible. This was done to ensure that, after it was processed in the distribution building, the water would flow downhill into various sections of the city. For example, Pompeii's water distribution building was located near the Vesuvius Gate, at the town's highest point, some 111 feet (34 m) above its lowest point, at the Stabian Gate, lying about 2,460 feet (750 m) away.

The Aqua Claudia, pictured here in an engraving, was one of nine aqueducts that delivered more than 200 million gallons of fresh water to Rome every day. The bulk of the water used by Rome's inhabitants originated in nearby mountain springs.

When the water from the *specus* entered the distribution center, it flowed into a big, stone-lined holding tank. The one at Pompeii was a circular chamber 19 feet (5.8 m) across and 14.2 feet (4.3 m) deep, with service walkways running along its sides. This reservoir had two vital functions, the first of which was to clean the water as best as was possible at the time. Although it had been taken from clear mountain springs, the unprocessed liquid still contained small traces of sand, pollen, and other residues and impurities.

One of the two purification methods the Romans employed was filtration. They placed a metal screen featuring numerous tiny holes at the spot where the water channel entered the distribution center and one or more similar screens in other key points in the building. Once these devices had filtered out the biggest particles, the second purification method went to work. It consisted of one or more settling tanks located near the holding tank. Each settling tank was a large basin in which the water rested long enough for most of the remaining impurities to sink to the bottom. From time to time, workers emptied and cleaned these tanks.

Roman Water Pipes

The distribution center's other principal task was, as its name suggests, to distribute the sanitized water to the town's residents. To do this, the system's builders employed a network of pipes. These were made of bronze, ceramic tile, concrete, wood, and/or lead.

Each of these substances had its particular benefits and drawbacks for fashioning pipes. Bronze, for instance, was strong and durable, but it was also quite expensive. This made unguarded bronze pipes a frequent target of thieves. Meanwhile, as the late scholar L. Sprague de Camp pointed out, "wood rots and splits" and "tile and concrete, though durable, have but little strength in tension and so cannot withstand much pressure from inside." As a result, most of Rome's water pipes were made of lead. Lead pipes, de Camp continued, "were made by rolling a sheet of lead into a cylinder and soldering [joining] the edges. Small lead pipes, with an oval or elliptical cross-section, carried water from distributing points at the outlet of each aqueduct to the places where the water was to be used."[40]

Lead had several advantages for ancient pipe making. It was durable, able to withstand a lot of pressure, and flexible enough that it could easily be bent into whatever shape was needed. One disadvantage of using lead for water pipes was that in significant quantities it can be hazardous to human health. The Romans were aware of this at least by the first century BCE, as evidenced by the fact that Vitruvius mentioned it in his famous book. But for reasons that are now unclear, his warning and those of other ancient writers about the dangers of lead were largely ignored and eventually forgotten.

Roman engineers and builders later replaced many of the lead pipes that had been used in the water distribution systems with ceramic (pottery or earthenware) ones. This was not because of the dangers of lead, however. Rather, it was because over time the cost of lead rose too high to make it a practical alternative. Indeed, Vitruvius himself urged the use of ceramic pipes to keep costs down. "If we wish

 METHODS OF STEALING WATER

In his book about Rome's aqueducts, Frontinus cited some examples of theft from the water system. One approach was perpetrated by people who bought an existing house whose former owner had permission to divert water for private use. The new owner applied for and got permission to insert a new nozzle in a nearby reservoir. But when possible, he left the older nozzle in place. With access to two water taps, he used the water from one for his private needs and sold the water from the second one on the black market. Another method of cheating the system—called puncturing—was to bribe water commission employees to ignore the existence of illegal pipes running off the aqueducts. "There are extensive areas in various places," Frontinus wrote,

> where secret pipes run under the pavements all over the city. I discovered that these pipes are furnishing water by special branches to all those engaged in business in those localities through which the pipes ran, being [drilled] for that purpose here and there by the so-called "puncturers," when it came to pass that only a small quantity of water reached the places of public supply. How large an amount of water has been stolen in this manner, I estimate by means of the fact that a considerable quantity of lead has been brought in by the removal of [those illegal] pipes.

Sextus Julius Frontinus, *The Aqueducts of Rome*, in *The Stratagems and the Aqueducts of Rome*, trans. C.E. Bennett. Cambridge, MA: Harvard University Press, 1993, p. 447.

to employ a less expensive method" of pipe making, he said, "we must proceed as follows. Earthenware pipes are to be made not less than two inches thick, and so tongued that they may enter into and fit one another. The joints are to be coated with quicklime [a substance made by burning limestone] worked up with oil."[41]

The Public Fountains

Whatever material they were fashioned from, hundreds of pipes carried the aqueduct's water away from the distribution center. These branched out until there were thousands of pipes leading to various destinations in the city. On average, such pipes were buried to a depth of approximately 2 feet (61 cm).

Also, as might be expected, after leaving the *castellum aquae*, the pipes ran at a slight downward incline, continuing to take advantage of gravity's pull to ensure that the water moved in the desired direction. However, this created a significant dilemma that had to be overcome for the system to work. Namely, when one forces water into a small pipe and slants it downward, it causes pressure to build up inside. Left alone, that tube might burst. Or the water might blast outward in an uncontrollable stream from the end of the pipe.

To overcome this difficulty, the builders cleverly erected hollow brick or stone towers at various points in the city. Within each tower, the water pipes entered at the bottom and then rose directly upward for a number of feet (an amount that varied from tower to tower) to a tank at the top. Because the upward-moving water was going *against* gravity, instead of taking advantage of it, the water slowed down and the pressure in the pipes decreased.

Another set of pipes led outward and downward from the tower's tank, carrying the water to a number of final destinations. Some of it flowed to Rome's eleven large bathhouses and more than eight hundred small bathhouses. Another share went to shops, laundries,

> **WORDS IN CONTEXT**
> *insulae*
> *Multistory apartment buildings in ancient Rome.*

The remnants of a water pipe built by the ancient Romans can still be seen in Sicily. The Romans built a network of pipes using bronze, ceramic tile, wood, and lead.

restaurants, and other commercial outlets. The largest proportion of water went to the many public fountains that dotted a typical Roman city. These were not mainly for decoration, like most modern fountains tend to be. The primary purpose of the ancient ones was to supply a town's residents with the water they needed for drinking and cooking. The usual procedure was to walk to the closest fountain, fill up one's bucket or other container, and then lug it home. Trying to make this strenuous task easier, the builders spaced the fountains so that they were a maximum of 260 feet (79 m) apart. That meant that each family could acquire clean aqueduct water at a spot no more than 130 feet (39.6 m) from the house or apartment where they resided.

Water Licenses

Not all of Rome's inhabitants had to undergo the arduous chore of carrying their water home each day. Just as the builders knew how to pipe water from the distribution center to the fountains, they were perfectly capable of sending it to sinks and faucets in individual homes. Most people did not enjoy that luxury, however, for two reasons. First, a majority of urban Romans dwelled in apartment buildings called *insulae*, which soared to heights of five or six and at times seven stories. Some of the shops and apartments on the ground floors of those structures *did* have running water that was piped in. Unfortunately for the rest of the residents, there was simply not enough pressure in the system to push the water to the upper floors. (The invention of plumbing systems with that kind of pressure lay many centuries in the future.)

The other problem was that, with certain exceptions, running pipes from the aqueducts directly to private residences was against the law since the government wanted to retain complete control over the water system. One of those exceptions consisted of the homes (at least, their ground floors) of the rich and famous. The imperial family, along with senators and military generals, were allowed to have their own private water lines. Many of these pipes led to outlets equipped with bronze faucets or taps similar to those in today's kitchens and bathrooms. Others who enjoyed private water lines were wealthy businessmen and a few other prominent individuals who received special permission.

This permission took the form of a written license. In his book, Frontinus reminded his readers that "no one shall draw water from the public supply without a license." Furthermore, he said, "whoever wishes to draw water for private use must seek for a grant and bring to the commissioner a writing [written permission] from the emperor." Frontinus added that "the right to granted water does not pass either to the heirs, or to the buyer [of the home], or to any new proprietor of the land."[42] This meant that the son of a person with a water license or someone who bought the home or land from that person was not covered by the license. He had to obtain his own.

Stealing from the Aqueducts

Frontinus also dutifully noted that there were people who failed to get a proper license and brazenly ignored the law. Some of them, he said, inserted nozzles into the holding tanks or other reservoirs connected to the aqueducts, siphoned off water, and sold it for a profit. Others secretly installed makeshift water lines from the aqueducts to their homes. He found that in some parts of the city, this kind of water theft, which he called "puncturing," was pervasive. There were large areas in which he discovered concealed pipes laid down just below the surface of the city streets all over the capital.

In addition, Frontinus said, in many cases the perpetrator of this illegal activity was in cahoots with one or more of the maintenance men who worked under him, individuals he referred to as "water men." They accepted regular bribes from the people who stole the water, agreeing to look the other way rather than report what was going on to their superiors.

Frontinus summarized the problem, asserting, "in the delivery of the water also it is manifest that there is fraud." Moreover, "the cause of this is the dishonesty of the water men, whom we have detected diverting water from the public conduits for private use. But a large number of landowners also, past whose fields the aqueducts run, tap the conduits." Indeed, he complained, "we have found irrigated fields, shops, garrets [houses of prostitution] even, and lastly all disorderly houses fitted up with fixtures [pipes and faucets], through which a constant supply of flowing water might be assured."[43]

Frontinus was well aware that there had long been a law against stealing water from the aqueducts. If convicted, a violator had to pay a large fine that was roughly equivalent to one hundred times the yearly salary of an average Roman soldier. In addition, the perpetrator was expected to repair all the damages he or she had caused to the aqueducts or other parts of the water system. Thanks to the survival of Frontinus's book, the actual wording of the law is known. In part, it said that anybody who "shall maliciously and intentionally" damage the "public waters," is a wrongdoer. That includes breaking, or even

Much of the water piped into Rome went to the city's many public fountains. The fountains provided water for drinking, cooking, and washing. Artwork from a later era depicts women washing clothes at Rome's Fountain of Minerva.

tolerating someone else's breaking, of "the channels, conduits, arches, pipes, tubes, reservoirs, or basins" of the aqueduct system. Whoever breaks the law "shall be condemned to pay a fine of 100,000 sesterces to the Roman people" and to "restore, reestablish, reconstruct, [or] replace what he has damaged."[44]

As a practical, realistic person, Frontinus recognized that by itself the law was not enough to stop all water theft. Constant vigilance was also needed. That is, the water men themselves, most of whom were honest, must keep a sharp eye out for efforts to cheat the system. "Frequent rounds must be made of the channels of the aqueducts outside the city," he wrote. "The same must be done in the case of reservoirs and public fountains" to ensure "that the water may flow without interruption, day and night."[45]

Aqueduct Maintenance and Repair

No evidence has survived to indicate how effective Frontinus and later water commissioners were at decreasing the incidence of theft of the public waters. What is more certain is that guarding against that crime was only one facet of the commissioner's job. Indeed, his primary task was to regularly repair and maintain the aqueducts and other aspects of the water system. Besides "the lawlessness of landowners living along the aqueducts,"[46] Frontinus pointed out, other reasons for repairs included the age of the aqueducts, periodic damage done by storms, and construction defects.

Most of the repair and maintenance work on the aqueducts, Frontinus stated, was done by specially trained slaves. These skilled individuals were divided into separate brigades or gangs. Rome's water commission had been established about a century before Frontinus's time by the first emperor, Augustus. The latter had appointed his close associate Marcus Agrippa to be the agency's first commissioner. Agrippa "kept his own private gang of slaves for the maintenance of the aqueducts and reservoirs and basins," Frontinus wrote. This unit of slaves was later "given to the state as its property by Augustus, who had received it in inheritance from Agrippa."[47]

In Frontinus's own day, he continued, there were two of those gangs, one belonging to the government and the other to the current emperor. The state-run gang consisted of about 240 men, whereas the emperor's group numbered 460. Further, each brigade was divided into specialized subgroups. According to Frontinus, they included "overseers, reservoir-keepers, inspectors, pavers, plasterers, and other workmen."[48] During an emergency, such as a major water leak, these well-trained professionals hurried to the scene and quickly effected repairs. If necessary, while they were working, they temporarily diverted water from other parts of the city to the neighborhood that had lost service.

Although these workers were slaves, few Roman occupations were more important than theirs. Maintaining the aqueducts, along with the roads, was absolutely vital to keeping up the high level of

SLAVES WITH SPECIAL STATUS

Fortunately for modern historians and history buffs, the always detail-oriented Frontinus mentioned who paid for the upkeep of the slaves in the water brigades. "The wages of the state gang," he wrote, "are paid from the state treasury," while the emperor's gang "gets its wages from the emperor's privy purse," meaning the imperial finance office. These slaves did not receive formal salaries or earnings in the modern sense. Their "wages" were a combination of the cost of housing and feeding them plus the tips, called *peculia*, they received for good behavior and hard work. The *peculia* of these special public slaves appear to have been unusually high compared to those of other slaves. This was likely because Roman leaders viewed their job—ensuring Rome a steady daily water supply—as absolutely vital, which thereby earned the slaves better-than-normal social status.

As the late scholar R.H. Barrow pointed out, the "water men enjoyed that superior social position" that most public servants enjoyed. This enhanced status allowed these slaves to marry free women, for instance. Evidence shows that water men named Epagathus, Sporus, and Sabbio all did so. (Their children were born as free Roman citizens.) Some water men also received promotions, including the gift of freedom. A man named Moschus, for example, began as an aqueduct slave and later became a free worker in the water commission's record office.

Sextus Julius Frontinus, *The Aqueducts of Rome*, in *The Stratagems and the Aqueducts of Rome*, trans. C.E. Bennett. Cambridge, MA: Harvard University Press, 1993, p. 449.

R.H. Barrow, *Slavery in the Roman Empire*. New York: Barnes and Noble, 1996, p. 140.

public services that the Empire's diverse residents had come to enjoy. Indeed, a major part of Rome's ability to preserve its hold on the peoples it had conquered over the centuries consisted of the unique engineering achievements that created those services.

In this way Rome's majestic system of roads and aqueducts helped to bring about and perpetuate an enormous realm that offered its inhabitants a remarkable degree of security, conveniences, and comforts. In the second century CE, when the Empire was at its zenith of power and culture, a Greek writer named Aelius Aristides recognized and praised the high level of civilization the Romans had produced. "Every place is full of gymnasia, fountains, gateways, temples, shops," he said, and "cities shine in radiance and beauty." Moreover, by using Rome's great network of roads, "Greek and non-Greek can now readily go wherever they please, with their property or without it." While erecting both roads and aqueducts, the Romans "have surveyed the whole world" and "built bridges of all sorts across rivers." With an extra flourish, Aristides further flattered his Roman audience, saying, "Those outside your Empire are fit to be pitied for losing such blessings."[49]

CHAPTER FIVE

Eternal and Living Memorials

Rome's systems of roads and aqueducts turned out to be part of its mighty legacy to the world. Moreover, the ultimate fate of those structures and their varied survival today were in large degree dictated by the Roman Empire's own destiny. Beginning in the second half of the fourth century (the 300s CE), that vast domain underwent steady and rapid economic and military decline. There was also a serious crisis of leadership, since most of the remaining emperors were not up to the task of ruling and keeping intact such an immense realm.

Finally, in 476 CE the last emperor, Romulus Augustulus, was deposed. The traditional Roman imperial government ceased to exist, and in the long medieval era that followed, the scattered remnants of the Empire developed into small, culturally backward local kingdoms. Some of them eventually became the nuclei of larger monarchies that grew into France, England, and other modern nations.

Today the fact that these nations evolved from the once great Roman realm is evidenced in part by the large number of Roman monuments that still dot their landscapes. Some of the more prominent examples are the impressive remains of the roads and aqueducts. Briefly tracing their individual fortunes and survival over the centuries reveals the significant influences of Roman culture and technology on later societies, including those of modern Europe.

The Example of Britain

In the first few centuries following the Empire's demise, for example, the Roman roads remained in general use across Europe and neighboring regions. Typical of this pattern was Britain. Wracked by economic problems and military setbacks, Rome abandoned it in 410 CE, more than six decades before Romulus Augustulus was forced from his throne.

The roads the Romans had created in Britain continued to support local traffic there for a long time after this wrenching separation. Yet in a slow but steady manner, two forces worked to marginalize and in some cases erase several of these highways. One force consisted of the effects of weather and natural decay. As a result of the broken ties between Rome's central government and Britain, there was no longer any regular upkeep of the roads there. So storms, floods, earthquakes, and relentless erosion, not to mention people stealing paving stones to build newer structures, took an increasing toll. The second force was the growth of new villages and towns in Britain. This stimulated the creation of new roads, some of which people came to favor over the older Roman ones.

Commenting on the survival of Roman roads in Britain, the *Lancashire Antiquarian*, a British online journal, mentions both of these factors. During the early medieval centuries, it says, numerous Roman roads in Britain "were still in a good enough state of repair for daily use." In fact, it has been estimated that in this period, "a minimum of 10,000 miles of usable Roman roads were still in existence in one form or another" in Britain. "However, due to a lack of maintenance many bridges and river crossings had become too dangerous to use, eventually causing the roads to deviate from their original routes and for travelers to find other crossing points. New roadways would also have been needed to allow travel to and from the new major medieval towns such as Oxford, Coventry, and Plymouth."[50]

WORDS IN CONTEXT
deposed
Toppled or overthrown.

TROUBLE ON THE MODERN VIA APPIA

Since the 1990s Italian archaeologists and concerned citizens have complained about rising vandalism along some sections of the Via Appia. "There are acts of vandalism almost every night," complains Rita Paris, the Italian official who administers the surviving ancient road. She also complains about a rash of illegal construction projects that have defaced some of the ancient monuments in the area. According to the *New York Times*'s Elisabetta Povoledo, who interviewed Paris, these include "a plant nursery that had become a restaurant (without planning permission), a cistern that had morphed into a swimming pool, and new villas tacked onto ancient monuments. Several are rented out for wedding receptions or society balls, which makes for a steady stream of traffic."

The interview reveals that Italy's central government has had only moderate success in reducing these unwanted activities. This is because large areas along the road are either privately owned or administered by local town governments. So the federal authorities often encounter arguments over who should be in charge of investigations and security. One recent approach taken by the Italian Culture Ministry to remedy the situation has been to buy some of the properties lying along the Via Appia. The ministry then cleans up these plots and provides security for them.

Quoted in Elisabetta Povoledo, "Past Catches Up with the Queen of Roads," *New York Times*, April 5, 2008. www.nytimes.com.

Povoledo, "Past Catches Up with the Queen of Roads."

As this process continued, some of the early English kings recognized the importance of maintaining a good road system. To that end, in the 1280s King Edward I passed a law that called for keeping the main Roman roads in a decent state of repair. Many later monarchs did not follow up on this effort, however, so many of the old Roman highways continued to deteriorate. Nevertheless, some sections of them have survived. Plus, hundreds of miles of others indirectly survive because modern roads were built right on top of them, thereby preserving their original routes. This same scenario of medieval use, steady decay, and indirect survival occurred in France, Spain, Greece, Italy, and other former parts of the Roman Empire.

The Via Appia in the Past

Meanwhile, in Italy the famous Via Appia, today the best preserved of the old Roman highways, experienced a fate somewhat different from that of most British Roman roads. It also mirrored a scenario that unfolded in many other sectors of Europe. Not long after the imperial throne became vacant in 476, one of Rome's former military generals—Odoacer, of German descent—proclaimed himself king of Italy. Seventeen years later, another German ruler, Theodoric, killed Odoacer and turned Italy into a Germanic kingdom.

The Via Appia (pictured) continued to provide an important route for soldiers, traders, and others in the years after Rome's fall. But eventually, parts of the road fell into disrepair from neglect.

But though their leaders and the name of their homeland had changed, the surviving residents of Rome and much of Italy continued their lives as before. Trade and travel went on. So they still regularly used the old Roman roads, including the Via Appia.

Over the century or so that followed, however, various invasions and other upheavals shook the region. Eventually, most of the remaining inhabitants no longer identified themselves as Romans, and life in the region came to be centered in local villages and their surrounding territories. One result was that fewer people traveled very far. So many of the existing roads, some sections of the Via Appia among them, saw less use and steadily fell into disrepair.

Nevertheless, paved roads like the Via Appia were extremely well made. A number of the leaders of the medieval Italian kingdoms that rose and fell in subsequent centuries recognized their value for trade and military transport. So in occasional short bursts of activity, they sank funds into repairing them. This did not start to happen to the Via Appia in a big way until the late 1700s, when Pope Pius VI ordered his own spate of repairs.

Pride in Italy's Past

Still more major renovation of the Via Appia took place in the early twentieth century. Italy had finally become a united modern nation a few decades before, and Italian national pride was still taking hold among the populace. Many people looked back with equal pride at their roots in the great empire that had once ruled the known world. In their minds, the Via Appia, as a surviving remnant of ancient Rome, should be cherished and celebrated.

Such feelings were often expressed by modern Italian artists, including the renowned musical composer Ottorino Respighi. The last movement of his 1924 work *The Pines of Rome* was intended to depict the picturesque trees lining the ancient Via Appia. In the music, Respighi tried to invoke images of Roman soldiers marching along that grand highway on their way to conquer their enemies.

In an eerie and disturbing reflection of those well-meaning musical pictures, the Via Appia soon relived part of its past. In World War II (1939–1945), Italy allied itself with Adolf Hitler's Nazi Germany. When the United States, Britain, and the other Allies invaded Italy in 1943, German armies marched down the Via Appia to launch their counterattack. Hoping to erase such embarrassing memories, when the Italians hosted the Summer Olympics in 1960, they made the venerable old road the official track for the runners of the marathon event.

The Via Appia Today

Continued pride in their connection with ancient Rome eventually motivated the Italians to create a large park situated along the first few miles of the Via Appia. Dedicated in 1988, it is called the Regional Park of the Old Appian Way. On Sundays and holidays the road closes to traffic and becomes a huge pedestrian zone where people stroll, picnic, relax, and/or look at Roman ruins in hopes of connecting with their ancient past.

In fact, only a few such vestiges of the past have survived inside the park. Well beyond its boundaries, however, there are stretches of the Via Appia around which the countryside maintains much of its ancient atmosphere. According to British archaeologist Amanda Claridge, as one travels outside Rome's city limits, "the road finally acquires the picturesque character for which it was so famous"[51] in past ages.

Among the surviving artifacts in these areas are the remains of ancient villas where rich urban Romans enjoyed rural getaways. There are also altars where people once performed animal sacrifices. Of particular interest to tourists are some of the catacombs, or underground

THE AQUEDUCTS AND ROADS IN MUSIC

The partial survival of many of ancient Rome's monumental structures, including roads and aqueducts, has inspired numerous modern musical composers. The most famous example is the Italian composer and conductor Ottorino Respighi (1879–1936). He wrote three large-scale orchestral works depicting ancient Roman culture in its heyday. Two of these include tributes to the aqueducts and roads.

The earlier of the two pieces, *The Fountains of Rome*, was composed in 1916. It consists of four movements, each of which portrays one of Rome's magnificent fountains whose waters were (and in the case of one still are) supplied by the city's aqueducts. The first movement depicts the Valle Giulia Fountain at dawn; the second the Triton Fountain in the morning; the third the Trevi Fountain at noon; and the fourth the Villa Medici Fountain at sunset.

The Pines of Rome, produced in 1924, also has four movements. The fourth, titled *The Pines of the Appian Way*, captures the beauty of the trees along that ancient highway at dawn, as well as the fearsome tread of Roman soldiers on its pavement later in the day. Both works are still regularly performed by major and minor orchestras around the world.

passages, where widely despised Christians hid from the imperial authorities.

More than anything else, though, one sees stone or brick tombs, many of which housed the remains of well-to-do Romans. In one 2.5-mile (4 km) stretch of the road, Claridge states, "the roadsides are open, lined with pines and cypress trees and the ruins of tomb after tomb in all shapes and sizes. Most took the form of towers or houses or small temples, but there are some more cylindrical monuments." The most famous of these is the Tomb of Caecilia Metella, which measures 98 feet (30 m) across and 36 feet (11 m) high. "The panoramic view from the tomb's roof is spectacular," Claridge continues, including the breathtaking sight of "the aqueducts still marching across the plain through the suburbs of modern Rome."[52]

Like Their Remote Ancestors

Those aqueducts that long ago brought life-giving water to the city of Rome had their own eventful and at times surprising history during the past two millennia. Sextus Julius Frontinus died in about 103 CE, not long after finishing his detailed account of Rome's aqueducts. In the years that followed, the Roman capital gained just two more of these lengthy water channels. The Aqua Traiana began operation in 109 CE, and the Aqua Alexandriana in 206.

As long as the Roman Empire remained united and strong and the government was careful to maintain the aqueducts, they likely would have continued delivering water indefinitely. As all empires and nations eventually do, however, over time the Roman realm steadily lost its cohesion, declined, and ceased to exist. As a result, no more new aqueducts were constructed, and the existing ones increasingly lapsed into disrepair.

During the first five medieval centuries, the few and mostly impoverished inhabitants of Rome now and then repaired and tried to maintain some of the city's old aqueducts. Yet this work was disorganized and lacked sufficient financial backing. Moreover, there was usually little or no follow-up by the next generation. As a result, by the beginning of the second millennium (circa 1000 CE), all eleven of these once splendid structures were completely out of commission. As their remote ancestors had, most of the city's residents had to fall back on cisterns and the Tiber River's water for their washing, bathing, drinking, and cooking needs.

Long-Lived Aqueducts

The dramatic story of the Roman aqueducts was not over, however. Outside of the former Roman capital, a few of the water channels that had supplied cities in the imperial provinces remained in use all through the medieval period and beyond. One was the Valens Aqueduct, erected by the emperor Valens in Constantinople (modern-day Istanbul, Turkey) in the late 300s. At a length of 155 miles (250 km),

Part of the Via Appia now passes through a public park, used by Rome's residents for picnics, bicycling, strolling, and more. Ancient villas and altars still stand along some sections of the road.

it was the longest of all the ancient Roman aqueducts. It was out of operation for a brief period in the 600s after its water channel was severed during a siege. But following the repairs, regular maintenance resumed, so it remained in constant use until well into the 1700s. One of its imposing arcades still runs through the city, looming above the daily traffic that passes right under several of its tall arches.

The aqueduct at Segovia, Spain, built by the emperor Domitian in the late first century CE, had an even longer life span. It remained in operation until the early twentieth century. Regrettably, vibrations and air pollution from the motors of modern cars and trucks damaged the structure's magnificent two-tiered arcade. But thanks to a grant from a large corporation, in 2006 work began on a project that aims first to repair and then to maintain the aqueduct in the future.

Meanwhile, although the medieval city of Rome's eleven

aqueducts eventually stopped working by the eleventh century, most of their miles-long water channels were still intact. A number of them needed only the attention of people with the will, means, and energy to restore them to service. A good example is the Aqua Virgo, completed in 19 BCE during Augustus's reign. After it ceased to operate in the mid-medieval era, Pope Nicholas V carefully restored it in 1453. Renamed the Aqua Vergine, it also benefited from repairs by later popes and all the while continued to send water to Rome's renowned Trevi Fountain. Indeed, today, more than two thousand years after its creation, that same aqueduct supplies the fountain with some 2.8 million cubic feet (80,000 cu. m) of clear water each day.

Modern Tributes

Another way that Rome's ancient aqueducts have influenced today's Rome and other modern cities is by providing a model or blueprint for new water systems. In several instances during the twentieth and twenty-first centuries, contractors have laid down new pipes directly above the ancient water channels. The newer pipes use the concept of water pumped under high pressure. This differs, of course, from the ancient channels, which operated at low pressure by taking advantage of the natural force of gravity. Still, over the centuries the buildings and streets of medieval and modern Rome were constructed around the surviving aqueduct arcades that snaked through the city. So in many cases they remain the most logical routes for water pipes to take.

Another modern tribute to the ancient aqueducts is the Parco Acquedotti, or Park of the Aqueducts. Centered some 5 miles (8 km) outside of Rome's city center, it prominently features sections of the Aqua Claudia. The massive surviving arches of that structure, which once carried 581 gallons (2,200 L) of fresh water per second into Rome, remain an architectural marvel.

WORDS IN CONTEXT

Quo Vadis
In Latin, *"where are you going?"* Supposedly a question Saint Peter asked Jesus, it became the title of an 1895 novel that inspired three movies.

Traffic flows under the Valens Aqueduct in Istanbul, Turkey. At one time it was the longest of all the ancient Roman aqueducts.

Because of the park's beauty and impressive ruins, scenes from a number of modern films have been shot there. MGM's spectacular 1951 version of the novel *Quo Vadis*, about the emperor Nero's persecution of the early Christians, was a colorful example. Several images of the hero and others riding in chariots were shot in the park using the Aqua Claudia's best-preserved arches as a backdrop. Probably the most famous movie scene shot there was the opening of Federico Fellini's 1960 masterpiece *La Dolce Vita*.

The Roman Spirit Survives

That people in the modern age make films about ancient Rome, as well as movies with modern themes that incorporate ancient Roman structures, is a testament to the greatness of that vanished civilization. Though the ancient Romans, along with their remarkable realm, are gone forever, their memory remains as vital as ever. This is due in no small part to the remains of thousands of Roman roads and aqueducts that still grace cities and rural landscapes across the Mediterranean world.

Part of the continuing allure of these structures is their outstanding practicality, a virtue that the Romans possessed in abundance. The remaining roads and aqueducts are also engaging because they reflect the extreme diligence and strong work ethic of their builders. As Edith Hamilton so aptly put it, they are surviving expressions of the ancient Roman spirit, with "its tremendous energy, and audacity, and pride."[53]

Most of all, however, these structures—among the finest ever produced by human minds and hands—remain riveting and important because of their sheer enormity. Rome "felt the need to display her power by a visible magnificence," Hamilton pointed out. "To the Roman, the big was itself admirable. The biggest temple in the world was as such better than the rest."[54] Another great scholar of ancient times, R.H. Barrow, phrased it another way. "Massive grandeur," he said, "is a mark of everything which the Romans constructed. They built for use and for permanence."[55]

Here, *permanence* is unarguably the operative word. Sections of many of the ancient Roman roads and aqueducts still stand, splendid and resolute. As long as people have the good sense to maintain them, they will remain eternal and in their own way living memorials to the talented engineers and industrious workers, both free and slave, who labored to erect them.

SOURCE NOTES

Introduction: Making a Great Empire Possible

1. Edith Hamilton, *The Roman Way to Western Civilization*. New York: Norton, 1993, p. 116.
2. Herodotus, *The Histories*, trans. Aubrey de Sélincourt. New York: Penguin, 1996, pp. 359–60.
3. Hamilton, *The Roman Way*, p. 156.
4. Jo-Ann Shelton, ed., *As the Romans Did: A Sourcebook in Roman Social History*, 2nd ed. New York: Oxford University Press, 1998, p. 68.
5. Strabo, *Geography*, trans. Jo-Ann Shelton, quoted in Shelton, *As the Romans Did*, p. 67.
6. Pliny the Elder, *Natural History*, excerpted in *Pliny the Elder: Natural History; A Selection*, trans. John H. Healy. New York: Penguin, 1991, p. 358.

Chapter One: To the Edges of the World

7. Strabo, *Geography*, p. 67.
8. Hamilton, *The Roman Way*, p. 116.
9. Siculus Flaccus, *On the Legal Status of Landholdings*, trans. Raymond Chevallier and N.H. Field, in *Roman Roads*, Raymond Chevallier. Berkeley: University of California Press, 1976, p. 65.
10. Livy, *History of Rome*, bks. 9 to 26, trans. D. Spillan and Cyrus Edmonds. Project Gutenberg e-book. www.gutenberg.org.
11. Shelton, *As the Romans Did*, p. 139.
12. Shelton, *As the Romans Did*, p. 139.
13. Flaccus, *On the Legal Status of Landholdings*, p. 65.
14. Quoted in Shelton, *As the Romans Did*, p. 330.
15. Chevallier, *Roman Roads*, p. 74.
16. L.A. Hamey and J.A. Hamey, *The Roman Engineers*. Cambridge: Cambridge University Press, 1981, p. 21.

17. Adam Hart-Davis, "Discovering Roman Technology," BBC, February 17, 2011. http://www.bbc.co.uk.

18. Hamey and Hamey, *The Roman Engineers*, p. 21.

19. Statius. *Silvae*. In *The Silvae of Statius*. Translated by D.A. Slater. Whitefish, MT: Kessenger, 2010, pp. 148–49.

Chapter Two: A Wide Array of Conveniences

20. Quoted in Chevallier, *Roman Roads*, p. 42.

21. Lionel Casson, *Travel in the Ancient World*. Baltimore, MD: Johns Hopkins University Press, 1994, p. 183.

22. Quoted in W.C. Firebaugh, *The Inns of Greece and Rome*. Whitefish, MT: Literary Licensing, 2012, p. 159.

23. Quoted in Philip Matyszak, *Ancient Rome on Five Denarii a Day*. New York: Thames and Hudson, 2007, p. 12.

24. Matyszak, *Ancient Rome on Five Denarii a Day*, pp. 12–13.

25. Casson, *Travel in the Ancient World*, p. 187.

26. Horace, *Satires*, in Shelton, *As The Romans Did*, pp. 327–28.

27. Chevallier, *Roman Roads*, p. 117.

Chapter Three: Providing Life-Giving Water

28. Shelton, *As the Romans Did*, p. 65.

29. Sextus Julius Frontinus, *The Aqueducts of Rome*, in *The Stratagems and the Aqueducts of Rome*, trans. C.E. Bennett. Cambridge, MA: Harvard University Press, 1993, pp. 357, 359.

30. Frontinus, *The Aqueducts of Rome*, p. 339.

31. Frontinus, *The Aqueducts of Rome*, p. 355.

32. Vitruvius, *On Architecture*, vol. 2, trans. Frank Granger. Cambridge, MA: Harvard University Press, 2002, pp. 137, 139.

33. Vitruvius, *On Architecture*, vol. 2, pp. 139, 141.

34. Vitruvius, *On Architecture*, vol. 2, p. 177.

35. Jean-Pierre Adam, *Roman Building: Materials and Techniques*, trans. Anthony Mathews. Bloomington: Indiana University Press, 2003, p. 241.

36. Hamey and Hamey, *The Roman Engineers*, p. 15.

37. Frontinus, *The Aqueducts of Rome*, p. 455.

Chapter Four: Flowing from Fountains and Faucets

38. Pliny the Elder, *Natural History*, p. 358.
39. Pliny the Elder, *Natural History*, p. 274.
40. L. Sprague de Camp, *The Ancient Engineers*. New York: Ballantine, 1995, p. 209.
41. Vitruvius, *On Architecture*, vol. 2, p. 87.
42. Frontinus, *The Aqueducts of Rome*, pp. 433, 435, 437, 441.
43. Frontinus, *The Aqueducts of Rome*, pp. 399, 405.
44. Frontinus, *The Aqueducts of Rome*, pp. 461, 463.
45. Frontinus, *The Aqueducts of Rome*, p. 435.
46. Frontinus, *The Aqueducts of Rome*, pp. 451, 453.
47. Frontinus, *The Aqueducts of Rome*, p. 429.
48. Frontinus, *The Aqueducts of Rome*, pp. 447, 449.
49. Aelius Aristides, *Roman Panegyric*, in *Roman Civilization, Sourcebook II: The Empire*, ed. Naphtali Lewis and Meyer Reinhold. New York: Harper and Row, 1966, p. 138.

Chapter Five: Eternal and Living Memorials

50. *Lancashire Antiquarian* (blog), "Medieval Roads = Roman Roads?," November 5, 2006. http://lancs99.blogspot.com.
51. Amanda Claridge, *Rome: An Oxford Archaeological Guide*. New York: Oxford University Press, 1998, p. 342.
52. Claridge, *Rome*, pp. 341–42.
53. Hamilton, *The Roman Way*, p. 157.
54. Hamilton, *The Roman Way*, p. 155.
55. R.H. Barrow. *The Romans*. New York: Penguin, 1985, p. 133.

FACTS ABOUT ROMAN ROADS AND AQUEDUCTS

Travel on Ancient Roads

- Persia's Royal Road ran for a distance of roughly 1,600 miles (2,575 km), from Susa in southern Iraq to Sardis in western Turkey.
- By about 300 CE the Roman Empire had more than 53,000 miles (85,295 km) of major roads.
- A courier traveling on the Roman highways covered an average of 45 miles (72 km) a day.
- The average distance between posting stations on the Roman roads was 9 miles (14.5 km).
- The average inn on an ancient Roman highway was about 70 feet (21 m) long and 40 feet (12 m) wide.
- The mules that lugged supplies along the Roman roads could carry an average of 450 pounds (204 kg) each.
- In comparison the donkeys that bore baggage along the Roman roads could carry an average of 250 pounds (113 kg) each.

Ancient Rome's Water System

- The longest aqueduct in the Roman realm was the Valens Aqueduct, which stretched 155 miles (250 km).
- The average amount that a Roman aqueduct's water channel inclined to take advantage of gravity was 2 to 3 feet (61 to 91 cm) per mile.
- The first aqueduct that served the city of Rome—the Aqua Appia—was about 10.5 miles (16.9 km) long.
- Together the eleven aqueducts that served the Roman capital ran for a total of 260 miles (418 km).
- The total output of the eleven aqueducts serving ancient Rome is estimated to have been 250 million gallons (946 million L) of water per day.

- In ancient Rome public water fountains were spaced about 260 feet (79 m) apart.
- The water distribution building in the Roman city of Pompeii was about 19 feet (5.8 m) in diameter.
- In the late first century CE, the fine for stealing water from the aqueducts was 100,000 *sesterces*, roughly one hundred times the average annual salary of a Roman soldier.
- In its prime the aqueduct called the Aqua Claudia carried 581 gallons (2,200 L) of water per second into the city of Rome.

Roman Roads and Aqueducts Today
- Approximately eight thousand milestones have been found along the surviving Roman roads.
- The Aqua Virgo, one of the eleven aqueducts serving the city of Rome, still supplies the Trevi Fountain with 2.8 million cubic feet (80,000 cu. m) of water each day.
- The Roman aqueduct known today as the Pont du Gard runs for 31 miles (50 km).
- The Roman aqueduct serving Segovia, in what is now Spain, is about 11 miles (17.7 km) long.

FOR FURTHER RESEARCH

Books

Tony Allan, *Exploring the Life, Myth, and Art of Ancient Rome*. New York: Rosen, 2011.

Horst Barow, *Roads and Bridges of the Roman Empire*. Fellbach, Germany: Axel Menges, 2013.

Simon James, *Ancient Rome*. London: Dorling Kindersley, 2011.

Carmelo Malacrino, *Constructing the Ancient World: Architectural Techniques of the Greeks and Romans*. Los Angeles: J. Paul Getty Museum, 2010.

Anthony Marks and Graham Tingay, *The Romans*. London: Usborne, 2013.

Nancy H. Ramage and Andrew Ramage, *Roman Art*. New York: Prentice-Hall, 2008.

Nigel Rodgers, *Roman Architecture*. Leicester, England: Anness, 2007.

John R. Senseny, *The Art of Building in the Classical World*. New York: Cambridge University Press, 2011.

John W. Stamper, *The Architecture of Roman Temples*. New York: Cambridge University Press, 2008.

Roger B. Ulrich and Caroline K. Quenemoen, eds., *A Companion to Roman Architecture*. Hoboken, NJ: Wiley-Blackwell, 2013.

Paul Zanker, *Roman Art*. trans. Henry Heitman-Gordon. Los Angeles: J. Paul Getty Museum, 2010.

Internet Sources

N.S. Gill, "Roman Roads," About.com, 2013. http://ancienthistory.about.com/od/romanroads/g/RomanRoads.htm.

Rabun Taylor, "How a Roman Aqueduct Works," *Archaeology*, March/April 2012. www.archive.archaeology.org/1203/features/how_a_roman_aqueduct_works.html.

Logan Thompson "Roman Roads," *History Today*, February 1997. www.historytoday.com/logan-thompson/roman-roads.

Mark Warner, "Roman Roads," Teaching Ideas. www.teachingideas.co.uk/history/romanrd.htm.

Fikret Yegul, "Roman Concrete," Roman Building Technology and Architecture. http://id-archserve.ucsb.edu/courses/arthistory/152k/concrete.html.

Websites

Ancient Roman Architecture, Great Buildings Online (http://www.greatbuildings.com/types/styles/roman.html). This site presents a useful list of links to articles about famous Roman structures, including many of the aqueducts and their imposing arcades.

Peutinger Map, Livius: Articles on Ancient History (www.livius.org/pen-pg/peutinger/map.html). An easy-to-read and informative page on the famous Roman map showing the Roman Empire's major highways; contains many useful links.

Typical Roman Stone Arch Construction, Technology Student.com (www.technologystudent.com/struct1/roman1.htm). Here, an expert uses both drawings and words to show how the piers and wedges of an arch were constructed.

Watering Ancient Rome, *Nova* (www.pbs.org/wgbh/nova/ancient /roman-aqueducts.html). Like other sites sponsored by PBS, this one about the Roman aqueducts is both well organized and enlightening.

INDEX

93

PICTURE CREDITS

Turkey, Istanbul, 4th-century Valens Aqueduct crossing Ataturk Bulvari, vehicles on busy road, cityscape visible through arches in background/Dorling Kindersley/UIG/The Bridgeman Art Library: 77

ABOUT THE AUTHOR

Historian Don Nardo is best known for his books for young people about the ancient and medieval worlds. These include histories of ancient Greece, Rome, Egypt, Mesopotamia, and medieval Europe, along with studies of ancient and medieval art and architecture, including Mesopotamian cities and literature, Egyptian sculpture and monuments, Greek temples, Roman amphitheaters and circuses, and medieval castles, sculpture, and painting. Nardo also composes and arranges orchestral music. He lives with his wife, Christine, in Massachusetts.

DATE DUE

BRODART, CO.   Cat. No. 23-221